This journal belongs to:

_____

_____

First Edition

ISBN: 9781670153081

Visit the author's website at LiveFreeAndThrive.space

Savoring with the 5 Senses:

A Chocolate Tasting Journal

Mena Borges-Gillette

Epigraph

Life is like chocolate: you should enjoy it piece for piece and
let it slowly melt on your tongue.
~ Nina Sandmann

True strength is when you can break a bar of chocolate into four pieces
with your bare hands — then just eat one.
~ Unknown

Save the earth it's the only planet with chocolate!
~ Unknown

Table of Contents

Introduction

This Tasting Journal was born from a chocolate history class I teach where we explore not only cacao's history, but also taste it in its various forms and make chocolate confections, both sweet and savory. One requirement of the university course is that students keep a tasting journal. I have put together rudimentary journals in the past but wanted a more elegant and comprehensive one that would also serve as a souvenir of the chocolates tasted in class as well as a steppingstone for future tastings. Because I did not find one that fit the bill on the market, I created this tasting journal.

The core of this journal consists of the sections "How to Savor Chocolate", "Guidelines for Hosting a Chocolate Tasting" and "How to Savor Chocolate Notes". The latter are preceded by basic information regarding cacao and chocolate including "A Brief Introduction to Cacao", "A Timeline of Cacao & Chocolate", "Chocolate Facts" and "Chocolate Quotes".

It is my hope that you will enjoy savoring chocolate with friends and family and that this journal may mark many celebratory occasions with "the food of the gods."

An Introduction to Theobroma cacao

Chocolate comes from the Theobroma cacao tree which demands a specific environment in order to grow. It only bears fruit at 20ºN - 20ºS longitude, at a low altitude and where the temperature is above 60ºF. The tree also demands year-round moisture, shade and humidity. It is susceptible to pod rots, wilts and fungus growths.

Theobroma cacao is an example of biological inefficiency. Its flower blossoms are pollenated exclusively by the midge fly. Of the hundreds of flowers produced by one cacao tree, only 1-3% bear fruit. Each flower results in a large pod containing 30-40 almond-shaped seeds or beans. Pods reach full growth in 4-5 months and take 1 month to ripen.

Cacao pods are hard to open, but squirrels, monkeys, and rats open them for their white pulp and thus avoid the seeds often dispersing them. The seed sprouts quickly and the resulting tree bears fruit in its third or fourth year.

The 3 types of cacao beans.

The noble **Criollo**; is referred to as "fine". Its chocolate has a distinctly reddish color and a complex taste which can include flavors of caramel, nuts, vanilla and tobacco. The Criollo tree is not resilient.

The common **Forastero** is considered the ordinary or bulk bean for mass production. The Forastero tree is hardy, robust and produces over 90% the of world's beans.

The **Trinitario** bean is the hybrid of the Criollo and Forastero varieties. In 1727, a hurricane in Trinidad caused Criollo trees to die of plant disease and were replaced by the Forastero. The Cross-pollination between these two varieties resulted in the Trinitario bean.

A Timeline of Cacao & Chocolate

• Cacao is said to have originated in the Amazon at least 4,000 years ago.

• **1500 BC - 400 BC** – The Olmecs in South America were the first to grow cacao as a domestic crop.

• **250 - 900 AD** – The Mayans make a drink from ground cacao beans, chilies and hot water which was unsweetened and made frothy by pouring the liquid from one vessel to another. The beverage was restricted to the society's elites. Cacao pods symbolized life and fertility for the Mayans and were often present in religious rituals and are referred to in their literature as "the food of gods".

- **14th Century** – The Mayans introduce the drink to the Aztecs who came to believe that the beverage had nourishing and fortifying qualities. It was therefore consumed by warriors for battle.
- **1502** – On his fourth voyage to the New World, Columbus encounters cacao beans being used as currency. He describes them as almonds.
- **1519** – Spanish explorer Hernán Cortéz did not like the cacao drink but was fascinated by the bean's value as currency. He established a plantation in the name of Spain, believing he could "grow" money.

  An example of the bean's value:

    1 bean = a tomato or a tamale

    3 beans = a turkey egg, an avocado, or a fish wrapped in maize husks

    100 full or 120 shrunken beans = a turkey hen or a rabbit

    200 beans = a turkey cock.

- **1528** – Cortéz returns to Spain and presents King Carlos V with beans from his plantation. It is after this introduction that the Spanish mix the bitter beverage with sugar, vanilla, nutmeg, cloves, allspice and cinnamon.
- **1570** – Chocolate gains popularity as a medicine.
- **1579** – **The Value of Chocolate Still a Secret:** After taking a Spanish ship loaded with cacao beans, English Buccaneers set it on fire thinking the beans were sheep dung.
- **1585** – The first official Spanish shipment of cacao beans arrives in Seville, Spain from Vera Cruz, México.
- **17th Century Catholic Church**: Religious leaders engage in discussions about whether chocolate is a beverage or a food and whether it breaks fast. Most people, including all consulted popes (from Gregory XIII - Benedict XIV) during the course of the debate agree that, since one drinks it, it does **not** break the fast.
- **1660s** – Chocolate gains popularity in **Italy**.
- **Mid - 1600s** – The **French** Court embraces chocolate when the Spanish Princess Maria Theresa is betrothed to Louis XIV of France. Chocolate's reputation as an aphrodisiac flourishes in French courts.
- **1650s - 1660s** – Chocolate's appearance in **England** coincides with the arrival of coffee from the Middle East and tea from China.
- **1657** – London's first chocolate house opens. They become trendy meeting places for the elite.

• **1674** – The first **solid chocolate** is introduced and is served in the form of chocolate rolls and cakes.

• **1730** – The steam engine brings mass production to chocolate. Cacao prices drop bringing it to within the reach of the masses.

• **1753** – The Swedish naturalist Linnaeus renames cacao "theobroma"; Greek for "food of the gods."

• **1819** – The pioneer chocolate-maker, François Louis **Callier**, opens the first Swiss chocolate factory.

• **1828** – Conrad **Van Houten** invents the cocoa press. Prices are cut. Chocolate quality improves by squeezing out some of the cacao butter, resulting in a smoother consistency. Van Houten also invents the process of treating cacao with alkali, giving it the name "Dutching".

• **1847** – Joseph **Fry & Son** develop a process of mixing some cacao butter back into the "Dutched" chocolate. They also add sugar, creating a paste that could be molded and hardened resulting the first modern chocolate bar.

• **1849** – **Ghirardelli** arrives in San Francisco for the Gold Rush but instead builds up his savings by selling tents to the miners and then starts his chocolate business.

• **1866** – The **Cadbury** Brothers, using Van Houten's press, introduce a new processing technique resulting in the launch of "Cadbury Cocoa Essence", the UK's first unadulterated cocoa. In 1879, the Cadburys build a factory town called Bournville and they express a concern for their workers. Cadbury's success is a result of mastering marketing.

• **1868** – Frenchman Etienne **Guittard** arrives in San Francisco in search of gold but starts a chocolate business instead. Today, Guittard, under control of its founder's great-grandson, Gary Guittard, is the largest privately-owned chocolate company in the United States.

• **1875** – After 8 years of development, Swiss chocolate maker Daniel **Peter** markets the first milk chocolate using condensed milk through Henri **Nestlé**'s process.

• **1879** – Rodolphe **Lindt** develops the technique of "conching". A process of rolling and heating chocolate for as much as 72 hours and adding cocoa butter. This makes the chocolate "fondant" allowing it to melt in the mouth.

1893 – Milton **Hershey** visits The Chicago's World Fair and is impressed by the chocolate processing machinery. He buys the machines to coat his candies with chocolate in his caramel manufacturing company. After a tour of chocolate manufacturers in Europe, he devotes his business to chocolate and rings in the 20th century by introducing the milk chocolate Hershey bar. In **1905**, he introduces the Hershey's Kiss. By **1906**, his enterprise is so vast that he takes over the town of Derry Church, renames it Hershey, Pennsylvania, and transforms it into the chocolate kingdom it is today. Until **1959**, when Fidel Castro seized power, Hershey also presided over "Hershey, Cuba" — a town he built around his sugar mill.

1908 – The Swiss chocolatier Jean **Tobler** introduces the triangular Toblerone bar.

1913 – Swiss chocolate maker Jules **Séchaud** develops a machine to fill chocolates thereby inventing the filled chocolate bonbon.

1922 – The French firm, **Valrhona** is founded. Today, their chocolates are among the few that use criollo variety cacao beans.

1926 – **Godiva**, the most famous purveyor of Belgian chocolates, is founded.

1941 – At Milton Hershey's suggestion —and in a move reminiscent of the Aztec practice— the U.S. Army begins including three 4-oz chocolate bars in soldiers' "D" rations. Meant to sustain the men, the bars came to be associated with the return of peace, when long-malnourished victims of the Germans found themselves approached by Americans holding out chocolate.

US FDA Standard of Identity

The US FDA Standard of Identity defines the percentages of key ingredients that must be present in each type of chocolate.

• **Chocolate Liquor:** ground or melted nib of the cacao bean in a smooth liquid state. It does not contain vegetable fat or alcohol. It may also be referred to as **chocolate, unsweetened chocolate, baking chocolate** or **bitter chocolate**.

• **Natural Cocoa Powder:** made by removing much of the fat (cocoa butter) and grinding the remaining material, excluding the shell, to a powder. Natural cocoa is not chemically treated.

• **Alkalized (Dutched) Cocoa Powder:** cocoa powder that is treated with an alkaline substance such as potassium carbonate to reduce acidity and darken the color. Alkalized cocoa powder must be identified as such in the nutrition label ingredient listing.

• **Semisweet (Bittersweet) Chocolate:** chocolate liquor with added cocoa butter and sugar. Must be at least 35 % chocolate liquor. Fat content may vary but averages between 30-35 %. Also referred to as **dark chocolate**.

• **Sweet Chocolate:** contains more sweeteners and cocoa butter than semisweet chocolate. Chocolate liquor content must be at least 15%.

• **Dark Chocolate:** This term is often used by consumers to describe both semisweet (bittersweet) & sweet chocolate as there is no defined standard of identity for regulatory purposes in the U.S. for "dark chocolate".

• **Milk Chocolate:** contains nutritive carbohydrate sweeteners, chocolate liquor, cocoa butter, milk (or cream) and flavors. Is composed of at least 10% chocolate liquor and 12% milk solids. The only fats allowed are cocoa butter and milk fat.

• **White Chocolate:** contains the same ingredients as milk chocolate but does not contain the nonfat portion of chocolate. Is composed of at least 20% cocoa butter, 14% total milk solids and less than 55% sweetener (sugar).

Chocolate Types Comparison Chart

Product	Chocolate Liquor	Milk Solids	Sugar	Cocoa Fat	Milk Fat
Milk Chocolate	≥ 10%	≥ 12%			
Sweet Chocolate	≥ 15%	< 12%			
Semi / Bittersweet (Dark) Chocolate	≥ 35%	< 12%			
White Chocolate		≥ 14%	≤ 55%	≥ 20%	≥ 3.5%

Chocolate Facts

• The word "chocolate" comes from the Aztec "cacahuatl" or "xocolatl," meaning "bitter water."

• The word "cocoa" was the result of the misspelling of "cacao."

• A cacao pod contains 30-40 beans. It takes 135-270 cocoa beans to make 1 pound of chocolate.

• Chocolate has over 500 individual flavor components.

• Although the myth has existed for generations, chocolate does not cause acne.

• One ounce of baking chocolate or cocoa contains 10% of the U.S. RDA of iron.

• 98% of the world's cacao is produced by just 15 countries.

• Cacao butter melts at slightly below normal body temperature, which is why chocolate will melt in the mouth.

• Per capita, Americans eat 12 pounds of chocolate annually. That is behind the Swiss, who eat 21 pounds per capita.

• Americans eat 2.8 billion pounds of chocolate annually, almost half the world's production.

• Americans spend $7 billion on chocolate annually.

• Over half the candy sold in the U.S. is chocolate.

• The theobromine in chocolate helps boost low blood-sugar levels.

Chocolate in Culture

As we have seen above, chocolate has had an immense impact on history. It even made a big impression on Thomas Jefferson even though his prediction may have been a bit off in a letter written to John Adams dated Nov 27, 1785: "Chocolate. [...] the superiority of the article [chocolate] both for health and nourishment will soon give it the same preference over tea & coffee in America which it has in Spain [...]" (http://tjrs.monticello.org/letter/1789). A little over one hundred years later, while Milton Hershey attended the 1893 World's Exposition in Chicago, he observed a chocolate-rolling machine being demonstrated and stated: "Caramels are only a fad. Chocolate is a permanent thing." (https://www.entrepeneur.com/article/197530)

In order to understand chocolate's impact on humanity and culture beyond history, reflecting on some ideas about the treat are the best illustration. For example, many people are aware of movies that either make a reference to it or pay homage to it such as Forest Gump's words. A less famous, but very pertinent phrase regarding how to enjoy chocolate is: "Chocolate should be savored, not rushed" which is found in Rick Riordan's *The Sword of Summer*. Other examples include the movies *Chocolat*, *Like Water for Chocolate*, *Willy Wonka and the Chocolate Factory*, etc. A cultural reference that merits reflection is found in Michael Pollan's *In Defense of Food: An Eater's Manifesto*: "He showed the words 'chocolate cake' to a group of Americans and recorded their word associations. 'Guilt' was the top response. If that strikes you as unexceptional, consider the response of French eaters to the same prompt: 'celebration.' Wow! The same food has very different meanings in different cultures which are serious and mirthful respectively. Chocolate also inspires the comedic ideas such as the phrase "If there's no chocolate in Heaven, I'm not going" found in Jane Seabrook's *Furry Logic Laugh at Life*. Chocolate is also seen as therapeutic in Geraldine Solon's *Chocolicious*, "May your life be filled, as mine has been, with love and laughter; and remember, when things are rough all you need is ... Chocolate." Chocolate is also referenced in J. K. Rowling's fictional infirmary in *Harry Potter and the Prisoner of Azkaban*: "'Well, he should have some chocolate, at the very least,' said Madam Pomfrey." And the phrase "Chocolate says 'I'm sorry' so much better than words" is found in Rachel Vincent's *My Soul to Save* if is one of emotional healing.

Other popular cultural references to chocolate abound in our digital age such as the following: The philosopher and poet, Henri Frederic Amiel, is credited with saying "Love is like swallowing hot chocolate before it has cooled off. It takes you by surprise at first, but keeps you warm for a long time." While author Amy Neftzger is credited with the funny: "I'm pretty sure that eating chocolate keeps wrinkles away because I have never seen a 10-year-old with a Hershey bar and crow's feet." The *Peanuts* comic strip's creator, Charles Schulz, has been credited with saying that "[e]xercise is a dirty word... Every time I hear it, I wash my mouth out with chocolate." He also had a twist on a famous song by a British boy band: "All you need is love. But a little chocolate now and then doesn't hurt."

Savoring Chocolate – Tips for getting started

• The chocolate should be at room temperature.

• In order to get the most out of the experience, avoid eating and drinking flavored beverages for 2 hours prior to your tasting. Arrange chocolate delicate to intense flavor, typically light to dark.

• In order to cleanse the palate between tastings, use water and plain crackers, bread or carrots.

• In order to cleanse any lingering aromas, breathe in coffee beans.

Savoring with the 5 Senses

1. Appearance – the look. Examine the chocolate's appearance.

• Describe the **color**:   Charcoal brown, Mocha, Caramel, Ivory

• Describe the appearance of the **surface**.

‣ Is it cloudy? Smooth? Shiny? Dull? Glossy? Waxy? Discolored? Does it have bubbles?

‣ Does the broken edge have an even color? A fine grain? Is it coarse? Crumbly? or stratified?

2. The Snap – the sound. Break off a piece of the chocolate listening to the sound.

• Does it break loudly, sharply or softly?

• Does it make an in between sound?

3. Aroma – the smell. Gently rub the chocolate between the fingers observing the texture as the aroma releases. Bring the chocolate to the nose in cupped hands, inhale its aromas.

• Terms to describe the **nose**.

Roasted:	Toast	Roasted Nuts	Mocha	Roasted Coffee		
Nutty:	Cashew	Pecan	Walnut	Macadamia	Pistachio	Almond Hazelnut
Caramels:	Toffee	Maple Syrup	Honey			
Dairy:	Yogurt	Buttery	Creamy			
Vanilla						
Fruity	Citrus:	Mandarin	Orange	Lemon	Lime	
	Berry:	Strawberry	Raspberry	Cherry	Grape	
	Tropical:	Coconut	Banana	Mango	Pineapple	
	Fruit:	Peach	Plum	Pear	Apple	
	Dried:	Apricot	Figs	Dates	Raisins	Prunes
Vegetal						
Earthy:	Olive	Mushrooms	Tobacco	Woodsy	Smoked Wood	Leather
Herbal:	Rosemary	Coriander				
Spice:	Pepper	Nutmeg	Ginger	Cinnamon	Clove	Licorice
Floral:	Jasmine	Violet	Rose	Lavender		

4. Texture – the mouthfeel: Allow it to melt on the tongue.

• Does it melt quickly or slowly?

• Does it feel smooth? Creamy? Greasy? Slimy?

• Is it hard or waxy? It is graining or gritty? Powdery?

Now chew and note the textures.

• Is the texture cakelike? Fudgy? Gummy? Sticky? Chewy?

5. Flavor / Finish – the taste. Allow the chocolate to melt on the tongue as it melts at body temperature. Softly chew allowing more flavor to release and enjoying the bouquet of flavors. Closing the eyes will allow you to continue to savor the layers of flavors that unfold.

• Does the flavor come quickly or slowly?

• Does it build & peak or remain constant?

• Does the flavor change character from the beginning to the middle to the end?

• Does the flavor last in the mouth or does it fade quickly?

• Is there any bitterness to the finish? Does it leave an aftertaste?

• Is the sweetness reminiscent of brown sugar? Molasses? Honey? Maple syrup? Caramel?

Another sweet substance? Is it pleasing or cloying (causing aversion)?

• Is the chocolate sweet, sour, bitter, salty, tart or acidic?

• Are there hints of vanilla? Herbs? Spices? Vegetal flavors? Tabaco?

• Are there hints of dried fruit? Wine? Tropical fruit? Citrus? Cherry? Plum? Other fruits?

• Are there hints of raw or roasted nut flavors? Roasted coffee?

• Are the flavors complex or simple? Balanced? Delicate? Muted? Intense?

• Term to describe the <u>flavor</u>.

Vegetal / Earthy:	woody, smoky, oaky, toasted grain, salt, tobacco, musty
Spiced / Nutty:	vanilla, ginger, cinnamon, licorice, clove, mint, pepper, any nut
Fruity:	berries, citrus, tropical fruit, dried fruit (cherry, raisin, plum)
Roasted:	coffee, cocoa, tea, caramel or burnt sugar, brown sugar
Dairy:	Cream, milk, buttery

Guidelines for Hosting a Chocolate Tasting

1. **Pick** chocolate and / or the chocolate theme.

2. **Sort** tasting by chocolate type. For example, if you are tasting dark and milk chocolate, place each in their group so that one type is savored at a time allowing for palate cleansing.

3. **Break** or cut samples into small pieces.

4. **Present** the chocolate by placing each type on a different platter or tray.

   For a blind tasting, remove the labels and place a number on the platter or tray. Use a master list that places the name of the chocolate next to its corresponding number.

5. **Savor** the chocolate at room temperature. If the chocolate is too cold, it will not melt in the mouth. If it is too warm, it will melt in the hands.

6. **Cleanse** the palate between chocolates with room temperature water and plain bread, crackers or carrots.

7. Following each bite, take the opportunity to write notes on your experience. Guests compare notes if desired.

How much chocolate?

Provide up to ½ oz. of each type of chocolate with 4 - 6 kinds per guest.

Professional chocolate tasters typically…

   …taste 1 type of chocolate at a time and no more than 6 at a sitting.

   …sit in a quiet room free of odor and may have dimmed lights.

   …do not speak while tasting leaving note comparing for afterward.

Those who taste chocolate for pleasure…

   …are flexible and may taste chocolates form a single brand or several; several chocolate types or only one.

   …tend to be more informal with the setting.

Chocolate Savoring Notes

DATE, OCCASION: _____   COMPANION(S): _____

CHOCOLATIER: _____   LOCATION: _____

CHOCOLATE NAME: _____

CACAO ORIGIN: _____   Cacao _____%

TYPE: □ Dark   □ Semi-Sweet   □ Milk   □ White

          □ Specialty Flavor: _____

Category: _____ (Bar, truffle, etc.)

Key Ingredients: _____

Allergy status. Contains: □ Gluten / Wheat   □ Milk

                              □ Soy   □ Eggs

                              □ Peanuts   □ Tree Nuts

                              □ Corn   □ Sesame

                              □ other: _____

Certifications: □ Fair-Trade   □ Rainforest Alliance

                    □ USDA Organic   □ Non-GMO Project

                    □ Gluten-Free   □ Kosher

                    □ Vegan   □ Paleo

Price: _____   Available at: _____

Label / Graphics: _____

_____

1. Appearance

Color: ☐ Charcoal Brown ☐ Mocha ☐ Caramel ☐ Ivory

Surface: ☐ Cloudy ☐ Smooth ☐ Shiny / Glossy ☐ Dull

☐ Molted ☐ Waxy ☐ Discolored ☐ Bubbles

☐ Even color ☐ Fine grain ☐ Coarse ☐ Crumbly ☐ Stratified

2. The Snap – the sound.

Breaks: ☐ Sharply (cracking) ☐ Loudly ☐ Quietly ☐ Softly

3. Aroma – the smell.

☐ Roasted: _____ ☐ Nutty: _____ ☐ Caramel: _____

☐ Dairy: _____ ☐ Vanilla: _____ ☐ Fruity: _____

☐ Vegetal: _____ ☐ Spice: _____ ☐ Floral: _____

4. Texture – Mouthfeel.

Melts: ☐ Quickly ☐ Slowly

Feels: ☐ Smooth ☐ Creamy ☐ Greasy ☐ Slimy

☐ Hard ☐ Waxy ☐ Graining ☐ Gritty ☐ Powdery

Texture: ☐ Cakelike ☐ Fudgy ☐ Gummy ☐ Sticky ☐ Chewy

5. Flavor & Finish

Flavor Intensity: ☐ DOA ☐ Subtle ☐ Bold

Flavor Profile: [Very sweet] 1 2 3 4 5 6 7 8 9 10 [Very bitter]

☐ sweet ☐ sour ☐ bitter ☐ salty ☐ umami/savory

Flavors: _____

_____

Finish: ☐ Fades quickly ☐ Lingers pleasantly ☐ Won't go away

Recommend for: _____

Notes: _____

_____

Eat it again? ☐ Can't pay me to ☐ Maybe ☐ Sure ☐ Yes, please!

Rating: ☆ ☆ ☆ ☆ ☆

Chocolate Savoring Notes

DATE, OCCASION: _____   COMPANION(S): _____

CHOCOLATIER: _____   LOCATION: _____

CHOCOLATE NAME: _____

CACAO ORIGIN: _____   Cacao _____%

TYPE: □ Dark   □ Semi-Sweet   □ Milk   □ White

        □ Specialty Flavor: _____

Category: _____ (Bar, truffle, etc.)

Key Ingredients: _____

Allergy status. Contains: □ Gluten / Wheat   □ Milk

                □ Soy   □ Eggs

                □ Peanuts   □ Tree Nuts

                □ Corn   □ Sesame

                □ other: _____

Certifications: □ Fair-Trade   □ Rainforest Alliance

                □ USDA Organic   □ Non-GMO Project

                □ Gluten-Free   □ Kosher

                □ Vegan   □ Paleo

Price: _____   **Available at:** _____

Label / Graphics: _____

_____

1. Appearance

Color: □ Charcoal Brown □ Mocha □ Caramel □ Ivory

Surface: □ Cloudy □ Smooth □ Shiny / Glossy □ Dull

□ Molted □ Waxy □ Discolored □ Bubbles

□ Even color □ Fine grain □ Coarse □ Crumbly □ Stratified

2. The Snap – the sound.

Breaks: □ Sharply (cracking) □ Loudly □ Quietly □ Softly

3. Aroma – the smell.

□ Roasted: _____ □ Nutty: _____ □ Caramel: _____

□ Dairy: _____ □ Vanilla: _____ □ Fruity: _____

□ Vegetal: _____ □ Spice: _____ □ Floral: _____

4. Texture – Mouthfeel.

Melts: □ Quickly □ Slowly

Feels: □ Smooth □ Creamy □ Greasy □ Slimy

□ Hard □ Waxy □ Graining □ Gritty □ Powdery

Texture: □ Cakelike □ Fudgy □ Gummy □ Sticky □ Chewy

5. Flavor & Finish

Flavor Intensity: □ DOA □ Subtle □ Bold

Flavor Profile: [Very sweet] 1 2 3 4 5 6 7 8 9 10 [Very bitter]

□ sweet □ sour □ bitter □ salty □ umami/savory

Flavors: _____

_____

Finish: □ Fades quickly □ Lingers pleasantly □ Won't go away

Recommend for: _____

Notes: _____

_____

Eat it again? □ Can't pay me to □ Maybe □ Sure □ Yes, please!

Rating: ☆ ☆ ☆ ☆ ☆

Chocolate Savoring Notes

DATE, OCCASION: _____   COMPANION(S): _____

CHOCOLATIER: _____   LOCATION: _____

CHOCOLATE NAME: _____

CACAO ORIGIN: _____   Cacao _____%

TYPE: □ Dark   □ Semi-Sweet   □ Milk   □ White

□ Specialty Flavor: _____

Category: _____ (Bar, truffle, etc.)

Key Ingredients: _____

Allergy status. Contains: □ Gluten / Wheat   □ Milk

□ Soy   □ Eggs

□ Peanuts   □ Tree Nuts

□ Corn   □ Sesame

□ other: _____

Certifications: □ Fair-Trade   □ Rainforest Alliance

□ USDA Organic   □ Non-GMO Project

□ Gluten-Free   □ Kosher

□ Vegan   □ Paleo

Price: _____   Available at: _____

Label / Graphics: _____

_____

1. Appearance

Color: □ Charcoal Brown □ Mocha □ Caramel □ Ivory

Surface: □ Cloudy □ Smooth □ Shiny / Glossy □ Dull

□ Molted □ Waxy □ Discolored □ Bubbles

□ Even color □ Fine grain □ Coarse □ Crumbly □ Stratified

2. The Snap – the sound.

Breaks: □ Sharply (cracking) □ Loudly □ Quietly □ Softly

3. Aroma – the smell.

□ Roasted: _____ □ Nutty: _____ □ Caramel: _____

□ Dairy: _____ □ Vanilla: _____ □ Fruity: _____

□ Vegetal: _____ □ Spice: _____ □ Floral: _____

4. Texture – Mouthfeel.

Melts: □ Quickly □ Slowly

Feels: □ Smooth □ Creamy □ Greasy □ Slimy

□ Hard □ Waxy □ Graining □ Gritty □ Powdery

Texture: □ Cakelike □ Fudgy □ Gummy □ Sticky □ Chewy

5. Flavor & Finish

Flavor Intensity: □ DOA □ Subtle □ Bold

Flavor Profile: [Very sweet] 1　2　3　4　5　6　7　8　9　10 [Very bitter]

□ sweet □ sour □ bitter □ salty □ umami / savory

Flavors: _____

_____

Finish: □ Fades quickly □ Lingers pleasantly □ Won't go away

Recommend for: _____

Notes: _____

_____

Eat it again? □ Can't pay me to □ Maybe □ Sure □ Yes, please!

Rating: ☆ ☆ ☆ ☆ ☆

Chocolate Savoring Notes

DATE, OCCASION: _____   COMPANION(S): _____

CHOCOLATIER: _____   LOCATION: _____

CHOCOLATE NAME: _____

CACAO ORIGIN: _____   Cacao _____%

TYPE: ☐ Dark   ☐ Semi-Sweet   ☐ Milk   ☐ White

             ☐ Specialty Flavor: _____

Category: _____ (Bar, truffle, etc.)

Key Ingredients: _____

Allergy status. Contains: ☐ Gluten / Wheat   ☐ Milk

                             ☐ Soy   ☐ Eggs

                             ☐ Peanuts   ☐ Tree Nuts

                             ☐ Corn   ☐ Sesame

                             ☐ other: _____

Certifications: ☐ Fair-Trade   ☐ Rainforest Alliance

                   ☐ USDA Organic   ☐ Non-GMO Project

                   ☐ Gluten-Free   ☐ Kosher

                   ☐ Vegan   ☐ Paleo

Price: _____   Available at: _____

Label / Graphics: _____

_____

1. Appearance

Color: □ Charcoal Brown   □ Mocha   □ Caramel   □ Ivory

Surface: □ Cloudy   □ Smooth   □ Shiny / Glossy   □ Dull

□ Molted   □ Waxy   □ Discolored   □ Bubbles

□ Even color   □ Fine grain   □ Coarse   □ Crumbly   □ Stratified

2. The Snap – the sound.

Breaks: □ Sharply (cracking)   □ Loudly   □ Quietly   □ Softly

3. Aroma – the smell.

□ Roasted: _____   □ Nutty: _____   □ Caramel: _____

□ Dairy: _____   □ Vanilla: _____   □ Fruity: _____

□ Vegetal: _____   □ Spice: _____   □ Floral: _____

4. Texture – Mouthfeel.

Melts: □ Quickly   □ Slowly

Feels: □ Smooth   □ Creamy   □ Greasy   □ Slimy

□ Hard   □ Waxy   □ Graining   □ Gritty   □ Powdery

Texture: □ Cakelike   □ Fudgy   □ Gummy   □ Sticky   □ Chewy

5. Flavor & Finish

Flavor Intensity: □ DOA   □ Subtle   □ Bold

Flavor Profile: [Very sweet] 1   2   3   4   5   6   7   8   9   10 [Very bitter]

□ sweet   □ sour   □ bitter   □ salty   □ umami/savory

Flavors: _____

_____

Finish: □ Fades quickly   □ Lingers pleasantly   □ Won't go away

Recommend for: _____

Notes: _____

_____

Eat it again?   □ Can't pay me to   □ Maybe   □Sure   □ Yes, please!

Rating: ☆ ☆ ☆ ☆ ☆

Chocolate Savoring Notes

DATE, OCCASION: _____   COMPANION(S): _____

CHOCOLATIER: _____   LOCATION: _____

CHOCOLATE NAME: _____

CACAO ORIGIN: _____   Cacao _____%

TYPE: □ Dark   □ Semi-Sweet   □ Milk   □ White

          □ Specialty Flavor: _____

Category: _____ (Bar, truffle, etc.)

Key Ingredients: _____

Allergy status. Contains: □ Gluten / Wheat   □ Milk

                                   □ Soy   □ Eggs

                                   □ Peanuts   □ Tree Nuts

                                   □ Corn   □ Sesame

                                   □ other: _____

Certifications: □ Fair-Trade   □ Rainforest Alliance

                        □ USDA Organic   □ Non-GMO Project

                        □ Gluten-Free   □ Kosher

                        □ Vegan   □ Paleo

Price: _____   Available at: _____

Label / Graphics: _____

_____

1. Appearance

Color: □ Charcoal Brown   □ Mocha   □ Caramel   □ Ivory

Surface: □ Cloudy   □ Smooth   □ Shiny / Glossy   □ Dull

           □ Molted   □ Waxy   □ Discolored   □ Bubbles

           □ Even color   □ Fine grain   □ Coarse   □ Crumbly   □ Stratified

2. The Snap – the sound.

Breaks: □ Sharply (cracking)   □ Loudly   □ Quietly   □ Softly

3. Aroma – the smell.

□ Roasted: _____   □ Nutty: _____   □ Caramel: _____

□ Dairy: _____   □ Vanilla: _____   □ Fruity: _____

□ Vegetal: _____   □ Spice: _____   □ Floral: _____

4. Texture – Mouthfeel.

Melts: □ Quickly   □ Slowly

Feels: □ Smooth   □ Creamy   □ Greasy   □ Slimy

        □ Hard   □ Waxy   □ Graining   □ Gritty   □ Powdery

Texture: □ Cakelike   □ Fudgy   □ Gummy   □ Sticky   □ Chewy

5. Flavor & Finish

Flavor Intensity: □ DOA   □ Subtle   □ Bold

Flavor Profile: [Very sweet] 1   2   3   4   5   6   7   8   9   10 [Very bitter]

           □ sweet   □ sour   □ bitter   □ salty   □ umami/savory

Flavors: _____

_____

Finish: □ Fades quickly   □ Lingers pleasantly   □ Won't go away

Recommend for: _____

Notes: _____

_____

Eat it again?   □ Can't pay me to   □ Maybe   □ Sure   □ Yes, please!

Rating: ☆ ☆ ☆ ☆ ☆

Chocolate Savoring Notes

DATE, OCCASION: _____   COMPANION(S): _____

CHOCOLATIER: _____   LOCATION: _____

CHOCOLATE NAME: _____

CACAO ORIGIN: _____   Cacao _____%

TYPE: □ Dark   □ Semi-Sweet   □ Milk   □ White

           □ Specialty Flavor: _____

Category: _____ (Bar, truffle, etc.)

Key Ingredients: _____

Allergy status. Contains: □ Gluten / Wheat   □ Milk

                                 □ Soy   □ Eggs

                                 □ Peanuts   □ Tree Nuts

                                 □ Corn   □ Sesame

                                 □ other: _____

Certifications: □ Fair-Trade   □Rainforest Alliance

                         □ USDA Organic   □ Non-GMO Project

                         □ Gluten-Free   □ Kosher

                         □ Vegan   □ Paleo

Price: _____   Available at: _____

Label / Graphics: _____

_____

1. Appearance

Color: ☐ Charcoal Brown   ☐ Mocha   ☐ Caramel   ☐ Ivory

Surface: ☐ Cloudy   ☐ Smooth   ☐ Shiny / Glossy   ☐ Dull

☐ Molted   ☐ Waxy   ☐ Discolored   ☐ Bubbles

☐ Even color   ☐ Fine grain   ☐ Coarse   ☐ Crumbly   ☐ Stratified

2. The Snap – the sound.

Breaks: ☐ Sharply (cracking)   ☐ Loudly   ☐ Quietly   ☐ Softly

3. Aroma – the smell.

☐ Roasted: _____   ☐ Nutty: _____   ☐ Caramel: _____

☐ Dairy: _____   ☐ Vanilla: _____   ☐ Fruity: _____

☐ Vegetal: _____   ☐ Spice: _____   ☐ Floral: _____

4. Texture – Mouthfeel.

Melts: ☐ Quickly   ☐ Slowly

Feels: ☐ Smooth   ☐ Creamy   ☐ Greasy   ☐ Slimy

☐ Hard   ☐ Waxy   ☐ Graining   ☐ Gritty   ☐ Powdery

Texture: ☐ Cakelike   ☐ Fudgy   ☐ Gummy   ☐ Sticky   ☐ Chewy

5. Flavor & Finish

Flavor Intensity: ☐ DOA   ☐ Subtle   ☐ Bold

Flavor Profile: [Very sweet] 1   2   3   4   5   6   7   8   9   10 [Very bitter]

☐ sweet   ☐ sour   ☐ bitter   ☐ salty   ☐ umami / savory

Flavors: _____

_____

Finish: ☐ Fades quickly   ☐ Lingers pleasantly   ☐ Won't go away

Recommend for: _____

Notes: _____

_____

Eat it again?   ☐ Can't pay me to   ☐ Maybe   ☐ Sure   ☐ Yes, please!

Rating: ☆ ☆ ☆ ☆ ☆

Chocolate Savoring Notes

DATE, OCCASION: _____   COMPANION(S): _____

CHOCOLATIER: _____   LOCATION: _____

CHOCOLATE NAME: _____

CACAO ORIGIN: _____   Cacao _____%

TYPE: □ Dark   □ Semi-Sweet   □ Milk   □ White

□ Specialty Flavor: _____

Category: _____ (Bar, truffle, etc.)

Key Ingredients: _____

Allergy status. Contains: □ Gluten / Wheat   □ Milk

□ Soy   □ Eggs

□ Peanuts   □ Tree Nuts

□ Corn   □ Sesame

□ other: _____

Certifications: □ Fair-Trade   □ Rainforest Alliance

□ USDA Organic   □ Non-GMO Project

□ Gluten-Free   □ Kosher

□ Vegan   □ Paleo

Price: _____   Available at: _____

Label / Graphics: _____

_____

1. Appearance

Color: □ Charcoal Brown □ Mocha □ Caramel □ Ivory

Surface: □ Cloudy □ Smooth □ Shiny / Glossy □ Dull

□ Molted □ Waxy □ Discolored □ Bubbles

□ Even color □ Fine grain □ Coarse □ Crumbly □ Stratified

2. The Snap – the sound.

Breaks: □ Sharply (cracking) □ Loudly □ Quietly □ Softly

3. Aroma – the smell.

□ Roasted: _____ □ Nutty: _____ □ Caramel: _____

□ Dairy: _____ □ Vanilla: _____ □ Fruity: _____

□ Vegetal: _____ □ Spice: _____ □ Floral: _____

4. Texture – Mouthfeel.

Melts: □ Quickly □ Slowly

Feels: □ Smooth □ Creamy □ Greasy □ Slimy

□ Hard □ Waxy □ Graining □ Gritty □ Powdery

Texture: □ Cakelike □ Fudgy □ Gummy □ Sticky □ Chewy

5. Flavor & Finish

Flavor Intensity: □ DOA □ Subtle □ Bold

Flavor Profile: [Very sweet] 1　2　3　4　5　6　7　8　9　10 [Very bitter]

□ sweet □ sour □ bitter □ salty □ umami/savory

Flavors: _____

_____

Finish: □ Fades quickly □ Lingers pleasantly □ Won't go away

Recommend for: _____

Notes: _____

_____

Eat it again? □ Can't pay me to □ Maybe □ Sure □ Yes, please!

Rating: ☆ ☆ ☆ ☆ ☆

Chocolate Savoring Notes

DATE, OCCASION: _____   COMPANION(S): _____

CHOCOLATIER: _____   LOCATION: _____

CHOCOLATE NAME: _____

CACAO ORIGIN: _____   Cacao _____%

TYPE: □ Dark   □ Semi-Sweet   □ Milk   □ White

           □ Specialty Flavor: _____

Category: _____ (Bar, truffle, etc.)

Key Ingredients: _____

Allergy status. Contains: □ Gluten / Wheat   □ Milk

                            □ Soy   □ Eggs

                            □ Peanuts   □ Tree Nuts

                            □ Corn   □ Sesame

                            □ other: _____

Certifications: □ Fair-Trade   □ Rainforest Alliance

                      □ USDA Organic   □ Non-GMO Project

                      □ Gluten-Free   □ Kosher

                      □ Vegan   □ Paleo

Price: _____   Available at: _____

Label / Graphics: _____

_____

1. Appearance

Color: ☐ Charcoal Brown ☐ Mocha ☐ Caramel ☐ Ivory

Surface: ☐ Cloudy ☐ Smooth ☐ Shiny / Glossy ☐ Dull

☐ Molted ☐ Waxy ☐ Discolored ☐ Bubbles

☐ Even color ☐ Fine grain ☐ Coarse ☐ Crumbly ☐ Stratified

2. The Snap – the sound.

Breaks: ☐ Sharply (cracking) ☐ Loudly ☐ Quietly ☐ Softly

3. Aroma – the smell.

☐ Roasted: _____ ☐ Nutty: _____ ☐ Caramel: _____

☐ Dairy: _____ ☐ Vanilla: _____ ☐ Fruity: _____

☐ Vegetal: _____ ☐ Spice: _____ ☐ Floral: _____

4. Texture – Mouthfeel.

Melts: ☐ Quickly ☐ Slowly

Feels: ☐ Smooth ☐ Creamy ☐ Greasy ☐ Slimy

☐ Hard ☐ Waxy ☐ Graining ☐ Gritty ☐ Powdery

Texture: ☐ Cakelike ☐ Fudgy ☐ Gummy ☐ Sticky ☐ Chewy

5. Flavor & Finish

Flavor Intensity: ☐ DOA ☐ Subtle ☐ Bold

Flavor Profile: [Very sweet] 1　2　3　4　5　6　7　8　9　10 [Very bitter]

☐ sweet ☐ sour ☐ bitter ☐ salty ☐ umami/savory

Flavors: _____

_____

Finish: ☐ Fades quickly ☐ Lingers pleasantly ☐ Won't go away

Recommend for: _____

Notes: _____

_____

Eat it again? ☐ Can't pay me to ☐ Maybe ☐ Sure ☐ Yes, please!

Rating: ☆ ☆ ☆ ☆ ☆

Chocolate Savoring Notes

DATE, OCCASION: _____   COMPANION(S):_____

CHOCOLATIER: _____   LOCATION: _____

CHOCOLATE NAME: _____

CACAO ORIGIN: _____   Cacao _____%

TYPE: ☐ Dark   ☐ Semi-Sweet   ☐ Milk   ☐ White

☐ Specialty Flavor: _____

Category: _____ (Bar, truffle, etc.)

Key Ingredients: _____

Allergy status. Contains: ☐ Gluten / Wheat   ☐ Milk

☐ Soy   ☐ Eggs

☐ Peanuts   ☐ Tree Nuts

☐ Corn   ☐ Sesame

☐ other: _____

Certifications: ☐ Fair-Trade   ☐ Rainforest Alliance

☐ USDA Organic   ☐ Non-GMO Project

☐ Gluten-Free   ☐ Kosher

☐ Vegan   ☐ Paleo

Price: _____   Available at: _____

Label / Graphics: _____

_____

1. Appearance

Color: ☐ Charcoal Brown ☐ Mocha ☐ Caramel ☐ Ivory

Surface: ☐ Cloudy ☐ Smooth ☐ Shiny / Glossy ☐ Dull

☐ Molted ☐ Waxy ☐ Discolored ☐ Bubbles

☐ Even color ☐ Fine grain ☐ Coarse ☐ Crumbly ☐ Stratified

2. The Snap – the sound.

Breaks: ☐ Sharply (cracking) ☐ Loudly ☐ Quietly ☐ Softly

3. Aroma – the smell.

☐ Roasted: _____ ☐ Nutty: _____ ☐ Caramel: _____

☐ Dairy: _____ ☐ Vanilla: _____ ☐ Fruity: _____

☐ Vegetal: _____ ☐ Spice: _____ ☐ Floral: _____

4. Texture – Mouthfeel.

Melts: ☐ Quickly ☐ Slowly

Feels: ☐ Smooth ☐ Creamy ☐ Greasy ☐ Slimy

☐ Hard ☐ Waxy ☐ Graining ☐ Gritty ☐ Powdery

Texture: ☐ Cakelike ☐ Fudgy ☐ Gummy ☐ Sticky ☐ Chewy

5. Flavor & Finish

Flavor Intensity: ☐ DOA ☐ Subtle ☐ Bold

Flavor Profile: [Very sweet] 1   2   3   4   5   6   7   8   9   10 [Very bitter]

☐ sweet ☐ sour ☐ bitter ☐ salty ☐ umami/savory

Flavors: _____

_____

Finish: ☐ Fades quickly ☐ Lingers pleasantly ☐ Won't go away

Recommend for: _____

Notes: _____

_____

Eat it again? ☐ Can't pay me to ☐ Maybe ☐ Sure ☐ Yes, please!

Rating: ☆ ☆ ☆ ☆ ☆

Chocolate Savoring Notes

DATE, OCCASION: _____   COMPANION(S): _____

CHOCOLATIER: _____   LOCATION: _____

CHOCOLATE NAME: _____

CACAO ORIGIN: _____   Cacao _____%

TYPE: □ Dark   □ Semi-Sweet   □ Milk   □ White

          □ Specialty Flavor: _____

Category: _____ (Bar, truffle, etc.)

Key Ingredients: _____

Allergy status. Contains: □ Gluten / Wheat   □ Milk

                     □ Soy   □ Eggs

                     □ Peanuts   □ Tree Nuts

                     □ Corn   □ Sesame

                     □ other: _____

Certifications: □ Fair-Trade   □Rainforest Alliance

                      □ USDA Organic   □ Non-GMO Project

                      □ Gluten-Free   □ Kosher

                      □ Vegan   □ Paleo

Price: _____   Available at: _____

Label / Graphics: _____

_____

1. Appearance

Color: □ Charcoal Brown   □ Mocha   □ Caramel   □ Ivory

Surface: □ Cloudy   □ Smooth   □ Shiny / Glossy   □ Dull

□ Molted   □ Waxy   □ Discolored   □ Bubbles

□ Even color   □ Fine grain   □ Coarse   □ Crumbly   □ Stratified

2. The Snap – the sound.

Breaks: □ Sharply (cracking)   □ Loudly   □ Quietly   □ Softly

3. Aroma – the smell.

□ Roasted: _____   □ Nutty: _____   □ Caramel: _____

□ Dairy: _____   □ Vanilla: _____   □ Fruity: _____

□ Vegetal: _____   □ Spice: _____   □ Floral: _____

4. Texture – Mouthfeel.

Melts: □ Quickly   □ Slowly

Feels: □ Smooth   □ Creamy   □ Greasy   □ Slimy

□ Hard   □ Waxy   □ Graining   □ Gritty   □ Powdery

Texture: □ Cakelike   □ Fudgy   □ Gummy   □ Sticky   □ Chewy

5. Flavor & Finish

Flavor Intensity: □ DOA   □ Subtle   □ Bold

Flavor Profile: [Very sweet] 1   2   3   4   5   6   7   8   9   10 [Very bitter]

□ sweet   □ sour   □ bitter   □ salty   □ umami/savory

Flavors: _____

_____

Finish: □ Fades quickly   □ Lingers pleasantly   □ Won't go away

Recommend for: _____

Notes: _____

_____

Eat it again?   □ Can't pay me to   □ Maybe   □Sure   □ Yes, please!

Rating: ☆ ☆ ☆ ☆ ☆

Chocolate Savoring Notes

DATE, OCCASION: _____   COMPANION(S): _____

CHOCOLATIER: _____   LOCATION: _____

CHOCOLATE NAME: _____

CACAO ORIGIN: _____   Cacao _____%

TYPE: □ Dark   □ Semi-Sweet   □ Milk   □ White

          □ Specialty Flavor: _____

Category: _____ (Bar, truffle, etc.)

Key Ingredients: _____

Allergy status. Contains: □ Gluten / Wheat   □ Milk

                            □ Soy   □ Eggs

                            □ Peanuts   □ Tree Nuts

                            □ Corn   □ Sesame

                            □ other: _____

Certifications: □ Fair-Trade   □Rainforest Alliance

                    □ USDA Organic   □ Non-GMO Project

                    □ Gluten-Free   □ Kosher

                    □ Vegan   □ Paleo

Price: _____   Available at: _____

Label / Graphics: _____

_____

1. Appearance

Color: □ Charcoal Brown   □ Mocha   □ Caramel   □ Ivory

Surface: □ Cloudy   □ Smooth   □ Shiny / Glossy   □ Dull

□ Molted   □ Waxy   □ Discolored   □ Bubbles

□ Even color   □ Fine grain   □ Coarse   □ Crumbly   □ Stratified

2. The Snap – the sound.

Breaks: □ Sharply (cracking)   □ Loudly   □ Quietly   □ Softly

3. Aroma – the smell.

□ Roasted: _____   □ Nutty: _____   □ Caramel: _____

□ Dairy: _____   □ Vanilla: _____   □ Fruity: _____

□ Vegetal: _____   □ Spice: _____   □ Floral: _____

4. Texture – Mouthfeel.

Melts: □ Quickly   □ Slowly

Feels: □ Smooth   □ Creamy   □ Greasy   □ Slimy

□ Hard   □ Waxy   □ Graining   □ Gritty   □ Powdery

Texture: □ Cakelike   □ Fudgy   □ Gummy   □ Sticky   □ Chewy

5. Flavor & Finish

Flavor Intensity: □ DOA   □ Subtle   □ Bold

Flavor Profile: [Very sweet] 1   2   3   4   5   6   7   8   9   10 [Very bitter]

□ sweet   □ sour   □ bitter   □ salty   □ umami/savory

Flavors: _____

_____

Finish: □ Fades quickly   □ Lingers pleasantly   □ Won't go away

Recommend for: _____

Notes: _____

_____

Eat it again?   □ Can't pay me to   □ Maybe   □Sure   □ Yes, please!

Rating: ☆ ☆ ☆ ☆ ☆

Chocolate Savoring Notes

DATE, OCCASION: _____   COMPANION(S): _____

CHOCOLATIER: _____   LOCATION: _____

CHOCOLATE NAME: _____

CACAO ORIGIN: _____   Cacao _____%

TYPE: □ Dark   □ Semi-Sweet   □ Milk   □ White

　　　　□ Specialty Flavor: _____

Category: _____ (Bar, truffle, etc.)

Key Ingredients: _____

Allergy status. Contains: □ Gluten / Wheat   □ Milk

　　　　　　　　　　　　　　□ Soy   □ Eggs

　　　　　　　　　　　　　　□ Peanuts   □ Tree Nuts

　　　　　　　　　　　　　　□ Corn   □ Sesame

　　　　　　　　　　　　　　□ other: _____

Certifications: □ Fair-Trade   □Rainforest Alliance

　　　　　　　　　□ USDA Organic   □ Non-GMO Project

　　　　　　　　　□ Gluten-Free   □ Kosher

　　　　　　　　　□ Vegan   □ Paleo

Price: _____   Available at: _____

Label / Graphics: _____

_____

1. Appearance

Color: ☐ Charcoal Brown   ☐ Mocha   ☐ Caramel   ☐ Ivory

Surface: ☐ Cloudy   ☐ Smooth   ☐ Shiny / Glossy   ☐ Dull

          ☐ Molted   ☐ Waxy   ☐ Discolored   ☐ Bubbles

          ☐ Even color   ☐ Fine grain   ☐ Coarse   ☐ Crumbly   ☐ Stratified

2. The Snap – the sound.

Breaks: ☐ Sharply (cracking)   ☐ Loudly   ☐ Quietly   ☐ Softly

3. Aroma – the smell.

☐ Roasted: _____   ☐ Nutty: _____   ☐ Caramel: _____

☐ Dairy: _____   ☐ Vanilla: _____   ☐ Fruity: _____

☐ Vegetal: _____   ☐ Spice: _____   ☐ Floral: _____

4. Texture – Mouthfeel.

Melts: ☐ Quickly   ☐ Slowly

Feels: ☐ Smooth   ☐ Creamy   ☐ Greasy   ☐ Slimy

        ☐ Hard   ☐ Waxy   ☐ Graining ☐ Gritty   ☐ Powdery

Texture: ☐ Cakelike   ☐ Fudgy   ☐ Gummy ☐ Sticky   ☐ Chewy

5. Flavor & Finish

Flavor Intensity: ☐ DOA   ☐ Subtle   ☐ Bold

Flavor Profile: [Very sweet] 1   2   3   4   5   6   7   8   9   10 [Very bitter]

                   ☐ sweet   ☐ sour   ☐ bitter   ☐ salty   ☐ umami/savory

Flavors: _____

_____

Finish: ☐ Fades quickly   ☐ Lingers pleasantly   ☐ Won't go away

Recommend for: _____

Notes: _____

_____

Eat it again?   ☐ Can't pay me to   ☐ Maybe   ☐Sure   ☐ Yes, please!

Rating: ☆ ☆ ☆ ☆ ☆

Chocolate Savoring Notes

DATE, OCCASION: _____   COMPANION(S): _____

CHOCOLATIER: _____   LOCATION: _____

CHOCOLATE NAME: _____

CACAO ORIGIN: _____   Cacao _____%

TYPE: □ Dark   □ Semi-Sweet   □ Milk   □ White

             □ Specialty Flavor: _____

Category: _____ (Bar, truffle, etc.)

Key Ingredients: _____

Allergy status. Contains: □ Gluten / Wheat   □ Milk

                                 □ Soy   □ Eggs

                                 □ Peanuts   □ Tree Nuts

                                 □ Corn   □ Sesame

                                 □ other: _____

Certifications: □ Fair-Trade   □Rainforest Alliance

                       □ USDA Organic   □ Non-GMO Project

                       □ Gluten-Free   □ Kosher

                       □ Vegan   □ Paleo

Price: _____   Available at: _____

Label / Graphics: _____

_____

1. Appearance

Color: □ Charcoal Brown □ Mocha □ Caramel □ Ivory

Surface: □ Cloudy □ Smooth □ Shiny / Glossy □ Dull

□ Molted □ Waxy □ Discolored □ Bubbles

□ Even color □ Fine grain □ Coarse □ Crumbly □ Stratified

2. The Snap – the sound.

Breaks: □ Sharply (cracking) □ Loudly □ Quietly □ Softly

3. Aroma – the smell.

□ Roasted: _____ □ Nutty: _____ □ Caramel: _____

□ Dairy: _____ □ Vanilla: _____ □ Fruity: _____

□ Vegetal: _____ □ Spice: _____ □ Floral: _____

4. Texture – Mouthfeel.

Melts: □ Quickly □ Slowly

Feels: □ Smooth □ Creamy □ Greasy □ Slimy

□ Hard □ Waxy □ Graining □ Gritty □ Powdery

Texture: □ Cakelike □ Fudgy □ Gummy □ Sticky □ Chewy

5. Flavor & Finish

Flavor Intensity: □ DOA □ Subtle □ Bold

Flavor Profile: [Very sweet] 1   2   3   4   5   6   7   8   9   10 [Very bitter]

□ sweet □ sour □ bitter □ salty □ umami/savory

Flavors: _____

_____

Finish: □ Fades quickly □ Lingers pleasantly □ Won't go away

Recommend for: _____

Notes: _____

_____

Eat it again? □ Can't pay me to □ Maybe □ Sure □ Yes, please!

Rating: ☆ ☆ ☆ ☆ ☆

Chocolate Savoring Notes

DATE, OCCASION: _____   COMPANION(S): _____

CHOCOLATIER: _____   LOCATION: _____

CHOCOLATE NAME: _____

CACAO ORIGIN: _____   Cacao _____%

TYPE: □ Dark   □ Semi-Sweet   □ Milk   □ White

         □ Specialty Flavor: _____

Category: _____ (Bar, truffle, etc.)

Key Ingredients: _____

Allergy status. Contains: □ Gluten / Wheat   □ Milk

                             □ Soy   □ Eggs

                             □ Peanuts   □ Tree Nuts

                             □ Corn   □ Sesame

                             □ other: _____

Certifications: □ Fair-Trade   □ Rainforest Alliance

                   □ USDA Organic   □ Non-GMO Project

                   □ Gluten-Free   □ Kosher

                   □ Vegan   □ Paleo

Price: _____   Available at: _____

Label / Graphics: _____

_____

1. Appearance

Color: ☐ Charcoal Brown　　☐ Mocha　　☐ Caramel　　☐ Ivory

Surface: ☐ Cloudy　　☐ Smooth　　☐ Shiny / Glossy　　　☐ Dull

☐ Molted　　☐ Waxy　　☐ Discolored　　　☐ Bubbles

☐ Even color　☐ Fine grain　☐ Coarse　　☐ Crumbly　　☐ Stratified

2. The Snap – the sound.

Breaks: ☐ Sharply (cracking)　　☐ Loudly　　☐ Quietly　　☐ Softly

3. Aroma – the smell.

☐ Roasted: _____　☐ Nutty: _____　☐ Caramel: _____

☐ Dairy: _____　☐ Vanilla: _____　☐ Fruity: _____

☐ Vegetal: _____　☐ Spice: _____　☐ Floral: _____

4. Texture – Mouthfeel.

Melts:　☐ Quickly　　☐ Slowly

Feels:　☐ Smooth　　☐ Creamy　　☐ Greasy　☐ Slimy

☐ Hard　　☐ Waxy　　☐ Graining　☐ Gritty　　☐ Powdery

Texture: ☐ Cakelike　　☐ Fudgy　　☐ Gummy　☐ Sticky　☐ Chewy

5. Flavor & Finish

Flavor Intensity:　　☐ DOA　　　☐ Subtle　　　　☐ Bold

Flavor Profile: [Very sweet] 1　2　3　4　5　6　7　8　9　10 [Very bitter]

☐ sweet　☐ sour　☐ bitter　☐ salty　☐ umami/savory

Flavors: _____

_____

Finish:　　☐ Fades quickly　　☐ Lingers pleasantly　　☐ Won't go away

Recommend for: _____

Notes: _____

_____

Eat it again?　　☐ Can't pay me to　　☐ Maybe　　☐Sure　　☐ Yes, please!

Rating:　☆ ☆ ☆ ☆ ☆

Chocolate Savoring Notes

DATE, OCCASION: _____   COMPANION(S): _____

CHOCOLATIER: _____   LOCATION: _____

CHOCOLATE NAME: _____

CACAO ORIGIN: _____   Cacao _____%

TYPE: □ Dark   □ Semi-Sweet   □ Milk   □ White

        □ Specialty Flavor: _____

Category: _____ (Bar, truffle, etc.)

Key Ingredients: _____

Allergy status. Contains: □ Gluten / Wheat   □ Milk

                              □ Soy   □ Eggs

                              □ Peanuts   □ Tree Nuts

                              □ Corn   □ Sesame

                              □ other: _____

Certifications: □ Fair-Trade   □ Rainforest Alliance

                    □ USDA Organic   □ Non-GMO Project

                    □ Gluten-Free   □ Kosher

                    □ Vegan   □ Paleo

Price: _____   Available at: _____

Label / Graphics: _____

_____

1. Appearance

Color: □ Charcoal Brown □ Mocha □ Caramel □ Ivory

Surface: □ Cloudy □ Smooth □ Shiny / Glossy □ Dull

□ Molted □ Waxy □ Discolored □ Bubbles

□ Even color □ Fine grain □ Coarse □ Crumbly □ Stratified

2. The Snap – the sound.

Breaks: □ Sharply (cracking) □ Loudly □ Quietly □ Softly

3. Aroma – the smell.

□ Roasted: _____ □ Nutty: _____ □ Caramel: _____

□ Dairy: _____ □ Vanilla: _____ □ Fruity: _____

□ Vegetal: _____ □ Spice: _____ □ Floral: _____

4. Texture – Mouthfeel.

Melts: □ Quickly □ Slowly

Feels: □ Smooth □ Creamy □ Greasy □ Slimy

□ Hard □ Waxy □ Graining □ Gritty □ Powdery

Texture: □ Cakelike □ Fudgy □ Gummy □ Sticky □ Chewy

5. Flavor & Finish

Flavor Intensity: □ DOA □ Subtle □ Bold

Flavor Profile: [Very sweet] 1   2   3   4   5   6   7   8   9   10 [Very bitter]

□ sweet □ sour □ bitter □ salty □ umami/savory

Flavors: _____

_____

Finish: □ Fades quickly □ Lingers pleasantly □ Won't go away

Recommend for: _____

Notes: _____

_____

Eat it again? □ Can't pay me to □ Maybe □ Sure □ Yes, please!

Rating: ☆ ☆ ☆ ☆ ☆

Chocolate Savoring Notes

DATE, OCCASION: _____ COMPANION(S): _____

CHOCOLATIER: _____ LOCATION: _____

CHOCOLATE NAME: _____

CACAO ORIGIN: _____ Cacao _____%

TYPE: □ Dark   □ Semi-Sweet   □ Milk   □ White

         □ Specialty Flavor: _____

Category: _____ (Bar, truffle, etc.)

Key Ingredients: _____

Allergy status. Contains: □ Gluten / Wheat   □ Milk

                                   □ Soy   □ Eggs

                                   □ Peanuts   □ Tree Nuts

                                   □ Corn   □ Sesame

                                   □ other: _____

Certifications: □ Fair-Trade   □Rainforest Alliance

                                   □ USDA Organic   □ Non-GMO Project

                                   □ Gluten-Free   □ Kosher

                                   □ Vegan   □ Paleo

Price: _____   Available at: _____

Label / Graphics: _____

_____

1. Appearance

Color: □ Charcoal Brown □ Mocha □ Caramel □ Ivory

Surface: □ Cloudy □ Smooth □ Shiny / Glossy □ Dull

□ Molted □ Waxy □ Discolored □ Bubbles

□ Even color □ Fine grain □ Coarse □ Crumbly □ Stratified

2. The Snap – the sound.

Breaks: □ Sharply (cracking) □ Loudly □ Quietly □ Softly

3. Aroma – the smell.

□ Roasted: _____ □ Nutty: _____ □ Caramel: _____

□ Dairy: _____ □ Vanilla: _____ □ Fruity: _____

□ Vegetal: _____ □ Spice: _____ □ Floral: _____

4. Texture – Mouthfeel.

Melts: □ Quickly □ Slowly

Feels: □ Smooth □ Creamy □ Greasy □ Slimy

□ Hard □ Waxy □ Graining □ Gritty □ Powdery

Texture: □ Cakelike □ Fudgy □ Gummy □ Sticky □ Chewy

5. Flavor & Finish

Flavor Intensity: □ DOA □ Subtle □ Bold

Flavor Profile: [Very sweet] 1 2 3 4 5 6 7 8 9 10 [Very bitter]

□ sweet □ sour □ bitter □ salty □ umami/savory

Flavors: _____

_____

Finish: □ Fades quickly □ Lingers pleasantly □ Won't go away

Recommend for: _____

Notes: _____

_____

Eat it again? □ Can't pay me to □ Maybe □ Sure □ Yes, please!

Rating: ☆ ☆ ☆ ☆ ☆

Chocolate Savoring Notes

DATE, OCCASION: _____   COMPANION(S):_____

CHOCOLATIER: _____   LOCATION: _____

CHOCOLATE NAME: _____

CACAO ORIGIN: _____   Cacao _____%

TYPE: ☐ Dark   ☐ Semi-Sweet   ☐ Milk   ☐ White

            ☐ Specialty Flavor: _____

Category: _____ (Bar, truffle, etc.)

Key Ingredients: _____

Allergy status. Contains: ☐ Gluten / Wheat   ☐ Milk

                            ☐ Soy   ☐ Eggs

                            ☐ Peanuts   ☐ Tree Nuts

                            ☐ Corn   ☐ Sesame

                            ☐ other: _____

Certifications: ☐ Fair-Trade   ☐ Rainforest Alliance

                            ☐ USDA Organic   ☐ Non-GMO Project

                            ☐ Gluten-Free   ☐ Kosher

                            ☐ Vegan   ☐ Paleo

Price: _____   Available at: _____

Label / Graphics: _____

_____

1. Appearance

Color: □ Charcoal Brown □ Mocha □ Caramel □ Ivory

Surface: □ Cloudy □ Smooth □ Shiny / Glossy □ Dull

□ Molted □ Waxy □ Discolored □ Bubbles

□ Even color □ Fine grain □ Coarse □ Crumbly □ Stratified

2. The Snap – the sound.

Breaks: □ Sharply (cracking) □ Loudly □ Quietly □ Softly

3. Aroma – the smell.

□ Roasted: _____ □ Nutty: _____ □ Caramel: _____

□ Dairy: _____ □ Vanilla: _____ □ Fruity: _____

□ Vegetal: _____ □ Spice: _____ □ Floral: _____

4. Texture – Mouthfeel.

Melts: □ Quickly □ Slowly

Feels: □ Smooth □ Creamy □ Greasy □ Slimy

□ Hard □ Waxy □ Graining □ Gritty □ Powdery

Texture: □ Cakelike □ Fudgy □ Gummy □ Sticky □ Chewy

5. Flavor & Finish

Flavor Intensity: □ DOA □ Subtle □ Bold

Flavor Profile: [Very sweet] 1 2 3 4 5 6 7 8 9 10 [Very bitter]

□ sweet □ sour □ bitter □ salty □ umami/savory

Flavors: _____

_____

Finish: □ Fades quickly □ Lingers pleasantly □ Won't go away

Recommend for: _____

Notes: _____

_____

Eat it again? □ Can't pay me to □ Maybe □Sure □ Yes, please!

Rating: ☆ ☆ ☆ ☆ ☆

Chocolate Savoring Notes

DATE, OCCASION: _____   COMPANION(S):_____

CHOCOLATIER: _____   LOCATION: _____

CHOCOLATE NAME: _____

CACAO ORIGIN: _____   Cacao _____%

TYPE: □ Dark   □ Semi-Sweet   □ Milk   □ White

□ Specialty Flavor: _____

Category: _____ (Bar, truffle, etc.)

Key Ingredients: _____

Allergy status. Contains: □ Gluten / Wheat   □ Milk

□ Soy   □ Eggs

□ Peanuts   □ Tree Nuts

□ Corn   □ Sesame

□ other: _____

Certifications: □ Fair-Trade   □Rainforest Alliance

□ USDA Organic   □ Non-GMO Project

□ Gluten-Free   □ Kosher

□ Vegan   □ Paleo

Price: _____   Available at: _____

Label / Graphics: _____

_____

1. Appearance

Color: ☐ Charcoal Brown   ☐ Mocha   ☐ Caramel   ☐ Ivory

Surface: ☐ Cloudy   ☐ Smooth   ☐ Shiny / Glossy   ☐ Dull

            ☐ Molted   ☐ Waxy   ☐ Discolored   ☐ Bubbles

            ☐ Even color   ☐ Fine grain   ☐ Coarse   ☐ Crumbly   ☐ Stratified

2. The Snap – the sound.

    Breaks: ☐ Sharply (cracking)   ☐ Loudly   ☐ Quietly   ☐ Softly

3. Aroma – the smell.

☐ Roasted: _____   ☐ Nutty: _____   ☐ Caramel: _____

☐ Dairy: _____   ☐ Vanilla: _____   ☐ Fruity: _____

☐ Vegetal: _____   ☐ Spice: _____   ☐ Floral: _____

4. Texture – Mouthfeel.

    Melts: ☐ Quickly   ☐ Slowly

    Feels: ☐ Smooth   ☐ Creamy   ☐ Greasy   ☐ Slimy

            ☐ Hard   ☐ Waxy   ☐ Graining   ☐ Gritty   ☐ Powdery

    Texture: ☐ Cakelike   ☐ Fudgy   ☐ Gummy   ☐ Sticky   ☐ Chewy

5. Flavor & Finish

Flavor Intensity: ☐ DOA   ☐ Subtle   ☐ Bold

Flavor Profile: [Very sweet] 1   2   3   4   5   6   7   8   9   10 [Very bitter]

            ☐ sweet   ☐ sour   ☐ bitter   ☐ salty   ☐ umami/savory

Flavors: _____

_____

Finish: ☐ Fades quickly   ☐ Lingers pleasantly   ☐ Won't go away

Recommend for: _____

Notes: _____

_____

Eat it again?   ☐ Can't pay me to   ☐ Maybe   ☐ Sure   ☐ Yes, please!

Rating: ☆ ☆ ☆ ☆ ☆

Chocolate Savoring Notes

DATE, OCCASION: _____   COMPANION(S): _____

CHOCOLATIER: _____ ·   LOCATION: _____

CHOCOLATE NAME: _____

CACAO ORIGIN: _____   Cacao _____%

TYPE: □ Dark   □ Semi-Sweet   □ Milk   □ White

            □ Specialty Flavor: _____

Category: _____ (Bar, truffle, etc.)

Key Ingredients: _____

Allergy status. Contains: □ Gluten / Wheat   □ Milk

                            □ Soy   □ Eggs

                            □ Peanuts   □ Tree Nuts

                            □ Corn   □ Sesame

                            □ other: _____

Certifications: □ Fair-Trade   □Rainforest Alliance

                      □ USDA Organic   □ Non-GMO Project

                      □ Gluten-Free   □ Kosher

                      □ Vegan   □ Paleo

Price: _____   Available at: _____

Label / Graphics: _____

_____

1. Appearance

Color: □ Charcoal Brown □ Mocha □ Caramel □ Ivory

Surface: □ Cloudy □ Smooth □ Shiny / Glossy □ Dull

□ Molted □ Waxy □ Discolored □ Bubbles

□ Even color □ Fine grain □ Coarse □ Crumbly □ Stratified

2. The Snap – the sound.

Breaks: □ Sharply (cracking) □ Loudly □ Quietly □ Softly

3. Aroma – the smell.

□ Roasted: _____ □ Nutty: _____ □ Caramel: _____

□ Dairy: _____ □ Vanilla: _____ □ Fruity: _____

□ Vegetal: _____ □ Spice: _____ □ Floral: _____

4. Texture – Mouthfeel.

Melts: □ Quickly □ Slowly

Feels: □ Smooth □ Creamy □ Greasy □ Slimy

□ Hard □ Waxy □ Graining □ Gritty □ Powdery

Texture: □ Cakelike □ Fudgy □ Gummy □ Sticky □ Chewy

5. Flavor & Finish

Flavor Intensity: □ DOA □ Subtle □ Bold

Flavor Profile: [Very sweet] 1 2 3 4 5 6 7 8 9 10 [Very bitter]

□ sweet □ sour □ bitter □ salty □ umami/savory

Flavors: _____

_____

Finish: □ Fades quickly □ Lingers pleasantly □ Won't go away

Recommend for: _____

Notes: _____

_____

Eat it again? □ Can't pay me to □ Maybe □ Sure □ Yes, please!

Rating: ☆ ☆ ☆ ☆ ☆

Chocolate Savoring Notes

DATE, OCCASION: _____   COMPANION(S): _____

CHOCOLATIER: _____   LOCATION: _____

CHOCOLATE NAME: _____

CACAO ORIGIN: _____   Cacao _____%

TYPE: □ Dark   □ Semi-Sweet   □ Milk   □ White

□ Specialty Flavor: _____

Category: _____ (Bar, truffle, etc.)

Key Ingredients: _____

Allergy status. Contains: □ Gluten / Wheat   □ Milk

□ Soy   □ Eggs

□ Peanuts   □ Tree Nuts

□ Corn   □ Sesame

□ other: _____

Certifications: □ Fair-Trade   □Rainforest Alliance

□ USDA Organic   □ Non-GMO Project

□ Gluten-Free   □ Kosher

□ Vegan   □ Paleo

Price: _____   Available at: _____

Label / Graphics: _____

_____

1. Appearance

Color: ☐ Charcoal Brown ☐ Mocha ☐ Caramel ☐ Ivory

Surface: ☐ Cloudy ☐ Smooth ☐ Shiny / Glossy ☐ Dull

☐ Molted ☐ Waxy ☐ Discolored ☐ Bubbles

☐ Even color ☐ Fine grain ☐ Coarse ☐ Crumbly ☐ Stratified

2. The Snap – the sound.

Breaks: ☐ Sharply (cracking) ☐ Loudly ☐ Quietly ☐ Softly

3. Aroma – the smell.

☐ Roasted: _____ ☐ Nutty: _____ ☐ Caramel: _____

☐ Dairy: _____ ☐ Vanilla: _____ ☐ Fruity: _____

☐ Vegetal: _____ ☐ Spice: _____ ☐ Floral: _____

4. Texture – Mouthfeel.

Melts: ☐ Quickly ☐ Slowly

Feels: ☐ Smooth ☐ Creamy ☐ Greasy ☐ Slimy

☐ Hard ☐ Waxy ☐ Graining ☐ Gritty ☐ Powdery

Texture: ☐ Cakelike ☐ Fudgy ☐ Gummy ☐ Sticky ☐ Chewy

5. Flavor & Finish

Flavor Intensity: ☐ DOA ☐ Subtle ☐ Bold

Flavor Profile: [Very sweet] 1 2 3 4 5 6 7 8 9 10 [Very bitter]

☐ sweet ☐ sour ☐ bitter ☐ salty ☐ umami/savory

Flavors: _____

_____

Finish: ☐ Fades quickly ☐ Lingers pleasantly ☐ Won't go away

Recommend for: _____

Notes: _____

_____

Eat it again? ☐ Can't pay me to ☐ Maybe ☐ Sure ☐ Yes, please!

Rating: ☆ ☆ ☆ ☆ ☆

Chocolate Savoring Notes

DATE, OCCASION: _____   COMPANION(S): _____

CHOCOLATIER: _____   LOCATION: _____

CHOCOLATE NAME: _____

CACAO ORIGIN: _____   Cacao _____%

TYPE: □ Dark   □ Semi-Sweet   □ Milk   □ White

             □ Specialty Flavor: _____

Category: _____ (Bar, truffle, etc.)

Key Ingredients: _____

Allergy status. Contains: □ Gluten / Wheat   □ Milk

                            □ Soy   □ Eggs

                            □ Peanuts   □ Tree Nuts

                            □ Corn   □ Sesame

                            □ other: _____

Certifications: □ Fair-Trade   □ Rainforest Alliance

                    □ USDA Organic   □ Non-GMO Project

                    □ Gluten-Free   □ Kosher

                    □ Vegan   □ Paleo

Price: _____   Available at: _____

Label / Graphics: _____

_____

1. Appearance

Color: □ Charcoal Brown   □ Mocha   □ Caramel   □ Ivory

Surface: □ Cloudy   □ Smooth   □ Shiny / Glossy   □ Dull

□ Molted   □ Waxy   □ Discolored   □ Bubbles

□ Even color   □ Fine grain   □ Coarse   □ Crumbly   □ Stratified

2. The Snap – the sound.

Breaks: □ Sharply (cracking)   □ Loudly   □ Quietly   □ Softly

3. Aroma – the smell.

□ Roasted: _____   □ Nutty: _____   □ Caramel: _____

□ Dairy: _____   □ Vanilla: _____   □ Fruity: _____

□ Vegetal: _____   □ Spice: _____   □ Floral: _____

4. Texture – Mouthfeel.

Melts: □ Quickly   □ Slowly

Feels: □ Smooth   □ Creamy   □ Greasy   □ Slimy

□ Hard   □ Waxy   □ Graining   □ Gritty   □ Powdery

Texture: □ Cakelike   □ Fudgy   □ Gummy   □ Sticky   □ Chewy

5. Flavor & Finish

Flavor Intensity: □ DOA   □ Subtle   □ Bold

Flavor Profile: [Very sweet] 1   2   3   4   5   6   7   8   9   10 [Very bitter]

□ sweet   □ sour   □ bitter   □ salty   □ umami/savory

Flavors: _____

_____

Finish: □ Fades quickly   □ Lingers pleasantly   □ Won't go away

Recommend for: _____

Notes: _____

_____

Eat it again?   □ Can't pay me to   □ Maybe   □ Sure   □ Yes, please!

Rating: ☆ ☆ ☆ ☆ ☆

Chocolate Savoring Notes

DATE, OCCASION: _____   COMPANION(S): _____

CHOCOLATIER: _____   LOCATION: _____

CHOCOLATE NAME: _____

CACAO ORIGIN: _____   Cacao _____%

TYPE: □ Dark   □ Semi-Sweet   □ Milk   □ White

□ Specialty Flavor: _____

Category: _____ (Bar, truffle, etc.)

Key Ingredients: _____

Allergy status. Contains: □ Gluten / Wheat   □ Milk

□ Soy   □ Eggs

□ Peanuts   □ Tree Nuts

□ Corn   □ Sesame

□ other: _____

Certifications: □ Fair-Trade   □ Rainforest Alliance

□ USDA Organic   □ Non-GMO Project

□ Gluten-Free   □ Kosher

□ Vegan   □ Paleo

Price: _____   Available at: _____

Label / Graphics: _____

_____

1. Appearance

Color: ☐ Charcoal Brown ☐ Mocha ☐ Caramel ☐ Ivory

Surface: ☐ Cloudy ☐ Smooth ☐ Shiny / Glossy ☐ Dull

☐ Molted ☐ Waxy ☐ Discolored ☐ Bubbles

☐ Even color ☐ Fine grain ☐ Coarse ☐ Crumbly ☐ Stratified

2. The Snap – the sound.

Breaks: ☐ Sharply (cracking) ☐ Loudly ☐ Quietly ☐ Softly

3. Aroma – the smell.

☐ Roasted: _____ ☐ Nutty: _____ ☐ Caramel: _____

☐ Dairy: _____ ☐ Vanilla: _____ ☐ Fruity: _____

☐ Vegetal: _____ ☐ Spice: _____ ☐ Floral: _____

4. Texture – Mouthfeel.

Melts: ☐ Quickly ☐ Slowly

Feels: ☐ Smooth ☐ Creamy ☐ Greasy ☐ Slimy

☐ Hard ☐ Waxy ☐ Graining ☐ Gritty ☐ Powdery

Texture: ☐ Cakelike ☐ Fudgy ☐ Gummy ☐ Sticky ☐ Chewy

5. Flavor & Finish

Flavor Intensity: ☐ DOA ☐ Subtle ☐ Bold

Flavor Profile: [Very sweet] 1   2   3   4   5   6   7   8   9   10 [Very bitter]

☐ sweet ☐ sour ☐ bitter ☐ salty ☐ umami/savory

Flavors: _____

_____

Finish: ☐ Fades quickly ☐ Lingers pleasantly ☐ Won't go away

Recommend for: _____

Notes: _____

_____

Eat it again? ☐ Can't pay me to ☐ Maybe ☐ Sure ☐ Yes, please!

Rating: ☆ ☆ ☆ ☆ ☆

Chocolate Savoring Notes

DATE, OCCASION: _____   COMPANION(S): _____

CHOCOLATIER: _____   LOCATION: _____

CHOCOLATE NAME: _____

CACAO ORIGIN: _____   Cacao _____%

TYPE: □ Dark   □ Semi-Sweet   □ Milk   □ White

             □ Specialty Flavor: _____

Category: _____ (Bar, truffle, etc.)

Key Ingredients: _____

Allergy status. Contains: □ Gluten / Wheat   □ Milk

                            □ Soy   □ Eggs

                            □ Peanuts   □ Tree Nuts

                            □ Corn   □ Sesame

                            □ other: _____

Certifications: □ Fair-Trade   □Rainforest Alliance

                       □ USDA Organic   □ Non-GMO Project

                       □ Gluten-Free   □ Kosher

                       □ Vegan   □ Paleo

Price: _____   Available at: _____

Label / Graphics: _____

_____

1. Appearance

Color: ☐ Charcoal Brown ☐ Mocha ☐ Caramel ☐ Ivory

Surface: ☐ Cloudy ☐ Smooth ☐ Shiny / Glossy ☐ Dull

☐ Molted ☐ Waxy ☐ Discolored ☐ Bubbles

☐ Even color ☐ Fine grain ☐ Coarse ☐ Crumbly ☐ Stratified

2. The Snap – the sound.

Breaks: ☐ Sharply (cracking) ☐ Loudly ☐ Quietly ☐ Softly

3. Aroma – the smell.

☐ Roasted: _____ ☐ Nutty: _____ ☐ Caramel: _____

☐ Dairy: _____ ☐ Vanilla: _____ ☐ Fruity: _____

☐ Vegetal: _____ ☐ Spice: _____ ☐ Floral: _____

4. Texture – Mouthfeel.

Melts: ☐ Quickly ☐ Slowly

Feels: ☐ Smooth ☐ Creamy ☐ Greasy ☐ Slimy

☐ Hard ☐ Waxy ☐ Graining ☐ Gritty ☐ Powdery

Texture: ☐ Cakelike ☐ Fudgy ☐ Gummy ☐ Sticky ☐ Chewy

5. Flavor & Finish

Flavor Intensity: ☐ DOA ☐ Subtle ☐ Bold

Flavor Profile: [Very sweet] 1 2 3 4 5 6 7 8 9 10 [Very bitter]

☐ sweet ☐ sour ☐ bitter ☐ salty ☐ umami/savory

Flavors: _____

_____

Finish: ☐ Fades quickly ☐ Lingers pleasantly ☐ Won't go away

Recommend for: _____

Notes: _____

_____

Eat it again? ☐ Can't pay me to ☐ Maybe ☐ Sure ☐ Yes, please!

Rating: ☆ ☆ ☆ ☆ ☆

Chocolate Savoring Notes

DATE, OCCASION: _____   COMPANION(S): _____

CHOCOLATIER: _____   LOCATION: _____

CHOCOLATE NAME: _____

CACAO ORIGIN: _____   Cacao _____%

TYPE: □ Dark   □ Semi-Sweet   □ Milk   □ White

             □ Specialty Flavor: _____

Category: _____ (Bar, truffle, etc.)

Key Ingredients: _____

Allergy status. Contains: □ Gluten / Wheat   □ Milk

                                   □ Soy   □ Eggs

                                   □ Peanuts   □ Tree Nuts

                                   □ Corn   □ Sesame

                                   □ other: _____

Certifications: □ Fair-Trade   □ Rainforest Alliance

                           □ USDA Organic   □ Non-GMO Project

                           □ Gluten-Free   □ Kosher

                           □ Vegan   □ Paleo

Price: _____   Available at: _____

Label / Graphics: _____

_____

1. Appearance

Color: ☐ Charcoal Brown   ☐ Mocha   ☐ Caramel   ☐ Ivory

Surface: ☐ Cloudy   ☐ Smooth   ☐ Shiny / Glossy   ☐ Dull

☐ Molted   ☐ Waxy   ☐ Discolored   ☐ Bubbles

☐ Even color ☐ Fine grain ☐ Coarse   ☐ Crumbly   ☐ Stratified

2. The Snap – the sound.

Breaks: ☐ Sharply (cracking)   ☐ Loudly   ☐ Quietly   ☐ Softly

3. Aroma – the smell.

☐ Roasted: _____   ☐ Nutty: _____   ☐ Caramel: _____

☐ Dairy: _____   ☐ Vanilla: _____   ☐ Fruity: _____

☐ Vegetal: _____   ☐ Spice: _____   ☐ Floral: _____

4. Texture – Mouthfeel.

Melts: ☐ Quickly   ☐ Slowly

Feels: ☐ Smooth   ☐ Creamy   ☐ Greasy   ☐ Slimy

☐ Hard   ☐ Waxy   ☐ Graining ☐ Gritty   ☐ Powdery

Texture: ☐ Cakelike   ☐ Fudgy   ☐ Gummy ☐ Sticky   ☐ Chewy

5. Flavor & Finish

Flavor Intensity: ☐ DOA   ☐ Subtle   ☐ Bold

Flavor Profile: [Very sweet] 1   2   3   4   5   6   7   8   9   10 [Very bitter]

☐ sweet ☐ sour   ☐ bitter ☐ salty   ☐ umami/savory

Flavors: _____

_____

Finish: ☐ Fades quickly   ☐ Lingers pleasantly   ☐ Won't go away

Recommend for: _____

Notes: _____

_____

Eat it again?   ☐ Can't pay me to   ☐ Maybe   ☐Sure   ☐ Yes, please!

Rating: ☆ ☆ ☆ ☆ ☆

Chocolate Savoring Notes

DATE, OCCASION: _____   COMPANION(S): _____

CHOCOLATIER: _____   LOCATION: _____

CHOCOLATE NAME: _____

CACAO ORIGIN: _____   Cacao _____%

TYPE: □ Dark   □ Semi-Sweet   □ Milk   □ White

□ Specialty Flavor: _____

Category: _____ (Bar, truffle, etc.)

Key Ingredients: _____

Allergy status. Contains: □ Gluten / Wheat   □ Milk

□ Soy   □ Eggs

□ Peanuts   □ Tree Nuts

□ Corn   □ Sesame

□ other: _____

Certifications: □ Fair-Trade   □Rainforest Alliance

□ USDA Organic   □ Non-GMO Project

□ Gluten-Free   □ Kosher

□ Vegan   □ Paleo

Price: _____   Available at: _____

Label / Graphics: _____

_____

1. Appearance

Color: □ Charcoal Brown □ Mocha □ Caramel □ Ivory

Surface: □ Cloudy □ Smooth □ Shiny / Glossy □ Dull

□ Molted □ Waxy □ Discolored □ Bubbles

□ Even color □ Fine grain □ Coarse □ Crumbly □ Stratified

2. The Snap – the sound.

Breaks: □ Sharply (cracking) □ Loudly □ Quietly □ Softly

3. Aroma – the smell.

□ Roasted: _____ □ Nutty: _____ □ Caramel: _____

□ Dairy: _____ □ Vanilla: _____ □ Fruity: _____

□ Vegetal: _____ □ Spice: _____ □ Floral: _____

4. Texture – Mouthfeel.

Melts: □ Quickly □ Slowly

Feels: □ Smooth □ Creamy □ Greasy □ Slimy

□ Hard □ Waxy □ Graining □ Gritty □ Powdery

Texture: □ Cakelike □ Fudgy □ Gummy □ Sticky □ Chewy

5. Flavor & Finish

Flavor Intensity: □ DOA □ Subtle □ Bold

Flavor Profile: [Very sweet] 1 2 3 4 5 6 7 8 9 10 [Very bitter]

□ sweet □ sour □ bitter □ salty □ umami/savory

Flavors: _____

_____

Finish: □ Fades quickly □ Lingers pleasantly □ Won't go away

Recommend for: _____

Notes: _____

_____

Eat it again? □ Can't pay me to □ Maybe □ Sure □ Yes, please!

Rating: ☆ ☆ ☆ ☆ ☆

Chocolate Savoring Notes

DATE, OCCASION: _____   COMPANION(S): _____

CHOCOLATIER: _____   LOCATION: _____

CHOCOLATE NAME: _____

CACAO ORIGIN: _____   Cacao _____%

TYPE: □ Dark   □ Semi-Sweet   □ Milk   □ White

                □ Specialty Flavor: _____

Category: _____ (Bar, truffle, etc.)

Key Ingredients: _____

Allergy status. Contains: □ Gluten / Wheat   □ Milk

                                □ Soy   □ Eggs

                                □ Peanuts   □ Tree Nuts

                                □ Corn   □ Sesame

                                □ other: _____

Certifications: □ Fair-Trade   □ Rainforest Alliance

                            □ USDA Organic   □ Non-GMO Project

                            □ Gluten-Free   □ Kosher

                            □ Vegan   □ Paleo

Price: _____   Available at: _____

Label / Graphics: _____

_____

1. Appearance

Color: □ Charcoal Brown □ Mocha □ Caramel □ Ivory

Surface: □ Cloudy □ Smooth □ Shiny / Glossy □ Dull

□ Molted □ Waxy □ Discolored □ Bubbles

□ Even color □ Fine grain □ Coarse □ Crumbly □ Stratified

2. The Snap – the sound.

Breaks: □ Sharply (cracking) □ Loudly □ Quietly □ Softly

3. Aroma – the smell.

□ Roasted: _____ □ Nutty: _____ □ Caramel: _____

□ Dairy: _____ □ Vanilla: _____ □ Fruity: _____

□ Vegetal: _____ □ Spice: _____ □ Floral: _____

4. Texture – Mouthfeel.

Melts: □ Quickly □ Slowly

Feels: □ Smooth □ Creamy □ Greasy □ Slimy

□ Hard □ Waxy □ Graining □ Gritty □ Powdery

Texture: □ Cakelike □ Fudgy □ Gummy □ Sticky □ Chewy

5. Flavor & Finish

Flavor Intensity: □ DOA □ Subtle □ Bold

Flavor Profile: [Very sweet] 1   2   3   4   5   6   7   8   9   10 [Very bitter]

□ sweet □ sour □ bitter □ salty □ umami/savory

Flavors: _____

_____

Finish: □ Fades quickly □ Lingers pleasantly □ Won't go away

Recommend for: _____

Notes: _____

_____

Eat it again? □ Can't pay me to □ Maybe □ Sure □ Yes, please!

Rating: ☆ ☆ ☆ ☆ ☆

Chocolate Savoring Notes

DATE, OCCASION: _____   COMPANION(S): _____

CHOCOLATIER: _____   LOCATION: _____

CHOCOLATE NAME: _____

CACAO ORIGIN: _____   Cacao _____%

TYPE: □ Dark   □ Semi-Sweet   □ Milk   □ White

           □ Specialty Flavor: _____

Category: _____ (Bar, truffle, etc.)

Key Ingredients: _____

Allergy status. Contains: □ Gluten / Wheat   □ Milk

                                 □ Soy   □ Eggs

                                 □ Peanuts   □ Tree Nuts

                                 □ Corn   □ Sesame

                                 □ other: _____

Certifications: □ Fair-Trade   □Rainforest Alliance

                                 □ USDA Organic   □ Non-GMO Project

                                 □ Gluten-Free   □ Kosher

                                 □ Vegan   □ Paleo

Price: _____   Available at: _____

Label / Graphics: _____

_____

1. Appearance

Color: □ Charcoal Brown □ Mocha □ Caramel □ Ivory

Surface: □ Cloudy □ Smooth □ Shiny / Glossy □ Dull

□ Molted □ Waxy □ Discolored □ Bubbles

□ Even color □ Fine grain □ Coarse □ Crumbly □ Stratified

2. The Snap – the sound.

Breaks: □ Sharply (cracking) □ Loudly □ Quietly □ Softly

3. Aroma – the smell.

□ Roasted: _____ □ Nutty: _____ □ Caramel: _____

□ Dairy: _____ □ Vanilla: _____ □ Fruity: _____

□ Vegetal: _____ □ Spice: _____ □ Floral: _____

4. Texture – Mouthfeel.

Melts: □ Quickly □ Slowly

Feels: □ Smooth □ Creamy □ Greasy □ Slimy

□ Hard □ Waxy □ Graining □ Gritty □ Powdery

Texture: □ Cakelike □ Fudgy □ Gummy □ Sticky □ Chewy

5. Flavor & Finish

Flavor Intensity: □ DOA □ Subtle □ Bold

Flavor Profile: [Very sweet] 1 2 3 4 5 6 7 8 9 10 [Very bitter]

□ sweet □ sour □ bitter □ salty □ umami/savory

Flavors: _____

_____

Finish: □ Fades quickly □ Lingers pleasantly □ Won't go away

Recommend for: _____

Notes: _____

_____

Eat it again? □ Can't pay me to □ Maybe □ Sure □ Yes, please!

Rating: ☆ ☆ ☆ ☆ ☆

Chocolate Savoring Notes

DATE, OCCASION: _____   COMPANION(S): _____

CHOCOLATIER: _____   LOCATION: _____

CHOCOLATE NAME: _____

CACAO ORIGIN: _____   Cacao _____%

TYPE: □ Dark   □ Semi-Sweet   □ Milk   □ White

             □ Specialty Flavor: _____

Category: _____ (Bar, truffle, etc.)

Key Ingredients: _____

Allergy status. Contains: □ Gluten / Wheat   □ Milk

                             □ Soy   □ Eggs

                             □ Peanuts   □ Tree Nuts

                             □ Corn   □ Sesame

                             □ other: _____

Certifications: □ Fair-Trade   □ Rainforest Alliance

                             □ USDA Organic   □ Non-GMO Project

                             □ Gluten-Free   □ Kosher

                             □ Vegan   □ Paleo

Price: _____   Available at: _____

Label / Graphics: _____

_____

1. Appearance

Color: ☐ Charcoal Brown ☐ Mocha ☐ Caramel ☐ Ivory

Surface: ☐ Cloudy ☐ Smooth ☐ Shiny / Glossy ☐ Dull

☐ Molted ☐ Waxy ☐ Discolored ☐ Bubbles

☐ Even color ☐ Fine grain ☐ Coarse ☐ Crumbly ☐ Stratified

2. The Snap – the sound.

Breaks: ☐ Sharply (cracking) ☐ Loudly ☐ Quietly ☐ Softly

3. Aroma – the smell.

☐ Roasted: _____ ☐ Nutty: _____ ☐ Caramel: _____

☐ Dairy: _____ ☐ Vanilla: _____ ☐ Fruity: _____

☐ Vegetal: _____ ☐ Spice: _____ ☐ Floral: _____

4. Texture – Mouthfeel.

Melts: ☐ Quickly ☐ Slowly

Feels: ☐ Smooth ☐ Creamy ☐ Greasy ☐ Slimy

☐ Hard ☐ Waxy ☐ Graining ☐ Gritty ☐ Powdery

Texture: ☐ Cakelike ☐ Fudgy ☐ Gummy ☐ Sticky ☐ Chewy

5. Flavor & Finish

Flavor Intensity: ☐ DOA ☐ Subtle ☐ Bold

Flavor Profile: [Very sweet] 1   2   3   4   5   6   7   8   9   10 [Very bitter]

☐ sweet ☐ sour ☐ bitter ☐ salty ☐ umami/savory

Flavors: _____

_____

Finish: ☐ Fades quickly ☐ Lingers pleasantly ☐ Won't go away

Recommend for: _____

Notes: _____

_____

Eat it again? ☐ Can't pay me to ☐ Maybe ☐ Sure ☐ Yes, please!

Rating: ☆ ☆ ☆ ☆ ☆

Chocolate Savoring Notes

DATE, OCCASION: _____ COMPANION(S): _____

CHOCOLATIER: _____ LOCATION: _____

CHOCOLATE NAME: _____

CACAO ORIGIN: _____ Cacao _____%

TYPE: □ Dark □ Semi-Sweet □ Milk □ White

□ Specialty Flavor: _____

Category: _____ (Bar, truffle, etc.)

Key Ingredients: _____

Allergy status. Contains: □ Gluten / Wheat □ Milk

□ Soy □ Eggs

□ Peanuts □ Tree Nuts

□ Corn □ Sesame

□ other: _____

Certifications: □ Fair-Trade □Rainforest Alliance

□ USDA Organic □ Non-GMO Project

□ Gluten-Free □ Kosher

□ Vegan □ Paleo

Price: _____ Available at: _____

Label / Graphics: _____

_____

1. Appearance

Color: □ Charcoal Brown   □ Mocha   □ Caramel   □ Ivory

Surface: □ Cloudy   □ Smooth   □ Shiny / Glossy   □ Dull

□ Molted   □ Waxy   □ Discolored   □ Bubbles

□ Even color   □ Fine grain   □ Coarse   □ Crumbly   □ Stratified

2. The Snap – the sound.

Breaks: □ Sharply (cracking)   □ Loudly   □ Quietly   □ Softly

3. Aroma – the smell.

□ Roasted: _____   □ Nutty: _____   □ Caramel: _____

□ Dairy: _____   □ Vanilla: _____   □ Fruity: _____

□ Vegetal: _____   □ Spice: _____   □ Floral: _____

4. Texture – Mouthfeel.

Melts: □ Quickly   □ Slowly

Feels: □ Smooth   □ Creamy   □ Greasy   □ Slimy

□ Hard   □ Waxy   □ Graining   □ Gritty   □ Powdery

Texture: □ Cakelike   □ Fudgy   □ Gummy   □ Sticky   □ Chewy

5. Flavor & Finish

Flavor Intensity: □ DOA   □ Subtle   □ Bold

Flavor Profile: [Very sweet] 1   2   3   4   5   6   7   8   9   10 [Very bitter]

□ sweet   □ sour   □ bitter   □ salty   □ umami/savory

Flavors: _____

_____

Finish: □ Fades quickly   □ Lingers pleasantly   □ Won't go away

Recommend for: _____

Notes: _____

_____

Eat it again?   □ Can't pay me to   □ Maybe   □ Sure   □ Yes, please!

Rating: ☆ ☆ ☆ ☆ ☆

Chocolate Savoring Notes

DATE, OCCASION: _____ COMPANION(S): _____

CHOCOLATIER: _____ LOCATION: _____

CHOCOLATE NAME: _____

CACAO ORIGIN: _____ Cacao _____%

TYPE: □ Dark   □ Semi-Sweet   □ Milk   □ White

□ Specialty Flavor: _____

Category: _____ (Bar, truffle, etc.)

Key Ingredients: _____

Allergy status. Contains: □ Gluten / Wheat   □ Milk

□ Soy   □ Eggs

□ Peanuts   □ Tree Nuts

□ Corn   □ Sesame

□ other: _____

Certifications: □ Fair-Trade   □Rainforest Alliance

□ USDA Organic   □ Non-GMO Project

□ Gluten-Free   □ Kosher

□ Vegan   □ Paleo

Price: _____   Available at: _____

Label / Graphics: _____

_____

1. Appearance

Color: ☐ Charcoal Brown   ☐ Mocha   ☐ Caramel   ☐ Ivory

Surface: ☐ Cloudy   ☐ Smooth   ☐ Shiny / Glossy   ☐ Dull

           ☐ Molted   ☐ Waxy   ☐ Discolored   ☐ Bubbles

           ☐ Even color   ☐ Fine grain   ☐ Coarse   ☐ Crumbly   ☐ Stratified

2. The Snap – the sound.

Breaks: ☐ Sharply (cracking)   ☐ Loudly   ☐ Quietly   ☐ Softly

3. Aroma – the smell.

☐ Roasted: _____   ☐ Nutty: _____   ☐ Caramel: _____

☐ Dairy: _____   ☐ Vanilla: _____   ☐ Fruity: _____

☐ Vegetal: _____   ☐ Spice: _____   ☐ Floral: _____

4. Texture – Mouthfeel.

Melts: ☐ Quickly   ☐ Slowly

Feels: ☐ Smooth   ☐ Creamy   ☐ Greasy   ☐ Slimy

         ☐ Hard   ☐ Waxy   ☐ Graining ☐ Gritty   ☐ Powdery

Texture: ☐ Cakelike   ☐ Fudgy   ☐ Gummy ☐ Sticky   ☐ Chewy

5. Flavor & Finish

Flavor Intensity: ☐ DOA   ☐ Subtle   ☐ Bold

Flavor Profile: [Very sweet] 1   2   3   4   5   6   7   8   9   10 [Very bitter]

                    ☐ sweet   ☐ sour   ☐ bitter   ☐ salty   ☐ umami/savory

Flavors: _____

_____

Finish: ☐ Fades quickly   ☐ Lingers pleasantly   ☐ Won't go away

Recommend for: _____

Notes: _____

_____

Eat it again?   ☐ Can't pay me to   ☐ Maybe   ☐Sure   ☐ Yes, please!

Rating: ☆ ☆ ☆ ☆ ☆

Chocolate Savoring Notes

DATE, OCCASION: _____   COMPANION(S): _____

CHOCOLATIER: _____   LOCATION: _____

CHOCOLATE NAME: _____

CACAO ORIGIN: _____   Cacao _____%

TYPE: □ Dark   □ Semi-Sweet   □ Milk   □ White

        □ Specialty Flavor: _____

Category: _____ (Bar, truffle, etc.)

Key Ingredients: _____

Allergy status. Contains: □ Gluten / Wheat   □ Milk

        □ Soy   □ Eggs

        □ Peanuts   □ Tree Nuts

        □ Corn   □ Sesame

        □ other: _____

Certifications: □ Fair-Trade   □ Rainforest Alliance

        □ USDA Organic   □ Non-GMO Project

        □ Gluten-Free   □ Kosher

        □ Vegan   □ Paleo

Price: _____   Available at: _____

Label / Graphics: _____

_____

1. Appearance

Color: □ Charcoal Brown □ Mocha □ Caramel □ Ivory

Surface: □ Cloudy □ Smooth □ Shiny / Glossy □ Dull

□ Molted □ Waxy □ Discolored □ Bubbles

□ Even color □ Fine grain □ Coarse □ Crumbly □ Stratified

2. The Snap – the sound.

Breaks: □ Sharply (cracking) □ Loudly □ Quietly □ Softly

3. Aroma – the smell.

□ Roasted: _____ □ Nutty: _____ □ Caramel: _____

□ Dairy: _____ □ Vanilla: _____ □ Fruity: _____

□ Vegetal: _____ □ Spice: _____ □ Floral: _____

4. Texture – Mouthfeel.

Melts: □ Quickly □ Slowly

Feels: □ Smooth □ Creamy □ Greasy □ Slimy

□ Hard □ Waxy □ Graining □ Gritty □ Powdery

Texture: □ Cakelike □ Fudgy □ Gummy □ Sticky □ Chewy

5. Flavor & Finish

Flavor Intensity: □ DOA □ Subtle □ Bold

Flavor Profile: [Very sweet] 1   2   3   4   5   6   7   8   9   10 [Very bitter]

□ sweet □ sour □ bitter □ salty □ umami/savory

Flavors: _____

_____

Finish: □ Fades quickly □ Lingers pleasantly □ Won't go away

Recommend for: _____

Notes: _____

_____

Eat it again? □ Can't pay me to □ Maybe □ Sure □ Yes, please!

Rating: ☆ ☆ ☆ ☆ ☆

Chocolate Savoring Notes

DATE, OCCASION: _____   COMPANION(S): _____

CHOCOLATIER: _____   LOCATION: _____

CHOCOLATE NAME: _____

CACAO ORIGIN: _____   Cacao _____%

TYPE: □ Dark   □ Semi-Sweet   □ Milk   □ White

          □ Specialty Flavor: _____

Category: _____ (Bar, truffle, etc.)

Key Ingredients: _____

Allergy status. Contains: □ Gluten / Wheat   □ Milk

                            □ Soy   □ Eggs

                            □ Peanuts   □ Tree Nuts

                            □ Corn   □ Sesame

                            □ other: _____

Certifications: □ Fair-Trade   □Rainforest Alliance

                            □ USDA Organic   □ Non-GMO Project

                            □ Gluten-Free   □ Kosher

                            □ Vegan   □ Paleo

Price: _____   Available at: _____

Label / Graphics: _____

_____

1. Appearance

Color: □ Charcoal Brown □ Mocha □ Caramel □ Ivory

Surface: □ Cloudy □ Smooth □ Shiny / Glossy □ Dull

□ Molted □ Waxy □ Discolored □ Bubbles

□ Even color □ Fine grain □ Coarse □ Crumbly □ Stratified

2. The Snap – the sound.

Breaks: □ Sharply (cracking) □ Loudly □ Quietly □ Softly

3. Aroma – the smell.

□ Roasted: _____ □ Nutty: _____ □ Caramel: _____

□ Dairy: _____ □ Vanilla: _____ □ Fruity: _____

□ Vegetal: _____ □ Spice: _____ □ Floral: _____

4. Texture – Mouthfeel.

Melts: □ Quickly □ Slowly

Feels: □ Smooth □ Creamy □ Greasy □ Slimy

□ Hard □ Waxy □ Graining □ Gritty □ Powdery

Texture: □ Cakelike □ Fudgy □ Gummy □ Sticky □ Chewy

5. Flavor & Finish

Flavor Intensity: □ DOA □ Subtle □ Bold

Flavor Profile: [Very sweet] 1   2   3   4   5   6   7   8   9   10 [Very bitter]

□ sweet □ sour □ bitter □ salty □ umami/savory

Flavors: _____

_____

Finish: □ Fades quickly □ Lingers pleasantly □ Won't go away

Recommend for: _____

Notes: _____

_____

Eat it again? □ Can't pay me to □ Maybe □ Sure □ Yes, please!

Rating: ☆ ☆ ☆ ☆ ☆

Chocolate Savoring Notes

DATE, OCCASION: _____   COMPANION(S): _____

CHOCOLATIER: _____   LOCATION: _____

CHOCOLATE NAME: _____

CACAO ORIGIN: _____   Cacao _____%

TYPE: □ Dark   □ Semi-Sweet   □ Milk   □ White

      □ Specialty Flavor: _____

Category: _____ (Bar, truffle, etc.)

Key Ingredients: _____

Allergy status. Contains: □ Gluten / Wheat   □ Milk

                             □ Soy   □ Eggs

                             □ Peanuts   □ Tree Nuts

                             □ Corn   □ Sesame

                             □ other: _____

Certifications: □ Fair-Trade   □Rainforest Alliance

                    □ USDA Organic   □ Non-GMO Project

                    □ Gluten-Free   □ Kosher

                    □ Vegan   □ Paleo

Price: _____   Available at: _____

Label / Graphics: _____

_____

1. Appearance

Color: □ Charcoal Brown □ Mocha □ Caramel □ Ivory

Surface: □ Cloudy □ Smooth □ Shiny / Glossy □ Dull

□ Molted □ Waxy □ Discolored □ Bubbles

□ Even color □ Fine grain □ Coarse □ Crumbly □ Stratified

2. The Snap – the sound.

Breaks: □ Sharply (cracking) □ Loudly □ Quietly □ Softly

3. Aroma – the smell.

□ Roasted: _____ □ Nutty: _____ □ Caramel: _____

□ Dairy: _____ □ Vanilla: _____ □ Fruity: _____

□ Vegetal: _____ □ Spice: _____ □ Floral: _____

4. Texture – Mouthfeel.

Melts: □ Quickly □ Slowly

Feels: □ Smooth □ Creamy □ Greasy □ Slimy

□ Hard □ Waxy □ Graining □ Gritty □ Powdery

Texture: □ Cakelike □ Fudgy □ Gummy □ Sticky □ Chewy

5. Flavor & Finish

Flavor Intensity: □ DOA □ Subtle □ Bold

Flavor Profile: [Very sweet] 1 2 3 4 5 6 7 8 9 10 [Very bitter]

□ sweet □ sour □ bitter □ salty □ umami/savory

Flavors: _____

_____

Finish: □ Fades quickly □ Lingers pleasantly □ Won't go away

Recommend for: _____

Notes: _____

_____

Eat it again? □ Can't pay me to □ Maybe □Sure □ Yes, please!

Rating: ☆ ☆ ☆ ☆ ☆

Chocolate Savoring Notes

DATE, OCCASION: _____   COMPANION(S): _____

CHOCOLATIER: _____   LOCATION: _____

CHOCOLATE NAME: _____

CACAO ORIGIN: _____   Cacao _____%

TYPE: □ Dark   □ Semi-Sweet   □ Milk   □ White

□ Specialty Flavor: _____

Category: _____ (Bar, truffle, etc.)

Key Ingredients: _____

Allergy status. Contains: □ Gluten / Wheat   □ Milk

□ Soy   □ Eggs

□ Peanuts   □ Tree Nuts

□ Corn   □ Sesame

□ other: _____

Certifications: □ Fair-Trade   □Rainforest Alliance

□ USDA Organic   □ Non-GMO Project

□ Gluten-Free   □ Kosher

□ Vegan   □ Paleo

Price: _____   Available at: _____

Label / Graphics: _____

_____

1. Appearance

Color: □ Charcoal Brown □ Mocha □ Caramel □ Ivory

Surface: □ Cloudy □ Smooth □ Shiny / Glossy □ Dull

□ Molted □ Waxy □ Discolored □ Bubbles

□ Even color □ Fine grain □ Coarse □ Crumbly □ Stratified

2. The Snap – the sound.

Breaks: □ Sharply (cracking) □ Loudly □ Quietly □ Softly

3. Aroma – the smell.

□ Roasted: _____ □ Nutty: _____ □ Caramel: _____

□ Dairy: _____ □ Vanilla: _____ □ Fruity: _____

□ Vegetal: _____ □ Spice: _____ □ Floral: _____

4. Texture – Mouthfeel.

Melts: □ Quickly □ Slowly

Feels: □ Smooth □ Creamy □ Greasy □ Slimy

□ Hard □ Waxy □ Graining □ Gritty □ Powdery

Texture: □ Cakelike □ Fudgy □ Gummy □ Sticky □ Chewy

5. Flavor & Finish

Flavor Intensity: □ DOA □ Subtle □ Bold

Flavor Profile: [Very sweet] 1   2   3   4   5   6   7   8   9   10 [Very bitter]

□ sweet □ sour □ bitter □ salty □ umami/savory

Flavors: _____

_____

Finish: □ Fades quickly □ Lingers pleasantly □ Won't go away

Recommend for: _____

Notes: _____

_____

Eat it again? □ Can't pay me to □ Maybe □ Sure □ Yes, please!

Rating: ☆ ☆ ☆ ☆ ☆

Chocolate Savoring Notes

DATE, OCCASION: _____   COMPANION(S): _____

CHOCOLATIER: _____   LOCATION: _____

CHOCOLATE NAME: _____

CACAO ORIGIN: _____   Cacao _____%

TYPE: □ Dark   □ Semi-Sweet   □ Milk   □ White

□ Specialty Flavor: _____

Category: _____ (Bar, truffle, etc.)

Key Ingredients: _____

Allergy status. Contains: □ Gluten / Wheat   □ Milk

□ Soy   □ Eggs

□ Peanuts   □ Tree Nuts

□ Corn   □ Sesame

□ other: _____

Certifications: □ Fair-Trade   □ Rainforest Alliance

□ USDA Organic   □ Non-GMO Project

□ Gluten-Free   □ Kosher

□ Vegan   □ Paleo

Price: _____   Available at: _____

Label / Graphics: _____

_____

1. Appearance

Color: ☐ Charcoal Brown   ☐ Mocha   ☐ Caramel   ☐ Ivory

Surface: ☐ Cloudy   ☐ Smooth   ☐ Shiny / Glossy   ☐ Dull

☐ Molted   ☐ Waxy   ☐ Discolored   ☐ Bubbles

☐ Even color ☐ Fine grain   ☐ Coarse   ☐ Crumbly   ☐ Stratified

2. The Snap – the sound.

Breaks: ☐ Sharply (cracking)   ☐ Loudly   ☐ Quietly   ☐ Softly

3. Aroma – the smell.

☐ Roasted: _____   ☐ Nutty: _____   ☐ Caramel: _____

☐ Dairy: _____   ☐ Vanilla: _____   ☐ Fruity: _____

☐ Vegetal: _____   ☐ Spice: _____   ☐ Floral: _____

4. Texture – Mouthfeel.

Melts: ☐ Quickly   ☐ Slowly

Feels: ☐ Smooth   ☐ Creamy   ☐ Greasy   ☐ Slimy

☐ Hard   ☐ Waxy   ☐ Graining ☐ Gritty   ☐ Powdery

Texture: ☐ Cakelike   ☐ Fudgy   ☐ Gummy ☐ Sticky   ☐ Chewy

5. Flavor & Finish

Flavor Intensity: ☐ DOA   ☐ Subtle   ☐ Bold

Flavor Profile: [Very sweet] 1   2   3   4   5   6   7   8   9   10 [Very bitter]

☐ sweet ☐ sour   ☐ bitter ☐ salty   ☐ umami/savory

Flavors: _____

_____

Finish: ☐ Fades quickly   ☐ Lingers pleasantly   ☐ Won't go away

Recommend for: _____

Notes: _____

_____

Eat it again?   ☐ Can't pay me to   ☐ Maybe   ☐Sure   ☐ Yes, please!

Rating: ☆ ☆ ☆ ☆ ☆

Chocolate Savoring Notes

DATE, OCCASION: _____ COMPANION(S): _____

CHOCOLATIER: _____ LOCATION: _____

CHOCOLATE NAME: _____

CACAO ORIGIN: _____ Cacao _____%

TYPE: □ Dark   □ Semi-Sweet   □ Milk   □ White

□ Specialty Flavor: _____

Category: _____ (Bar, truffle, etc.)

Key Ingredients: _____

Allergy status. Contains: □ Gluten / Wheat   □ Milk

□ Soy   □ Eggs

□ Peanuts   □ Tree Nuts

□ Corn   □ Sesame

□ other: _____

Certifications: □ Fair-Trade   □Rainforest Alliance

□ USDA Organic   □ Non-GMO Project

□ Gluten-Free   □ Kosher

□ Vegan   □ Paleo

Price: _____   Available at: _____

Label / Graphics: _____

_____

1. Appearance

Color: □ Charcoal Brown   □ Mocha   □ Caramel   □ Ivory

Surface: □ Cloudy   □ Smooth   □ Shiny / Glossy   □ Dull

□ Molted   □ Waxy   □ Discolored   □ Bubbles

□ Even color   □ Fine grain   □ Coarse   □ Crumbly   □ Stratified

2. The Snap – the sound.

Breaks: □ Sharply (cracking)   □ Loudly   □ Quietly   □ Softly

3. Aroma – the smell.

□ Roasted: _____   □ Nutty: _____   □ Caramel: _____

□ Dairy: _____   □ Vanilla: _____   □ Fruity: _____

□ Vegetal: _____   □ Spice: _____   □ Floral: _____

4. Texture – Mouthfeel.

Melts: □ Quickly   □ Slowly

Feels: □ Smooth   □ Creamy   □ Greasy   □ Slimy

□ Hard   □ Waxy   □ Graining   □ Gritty   □ Powdery

Texture: □ Cakelike   □ Fudgy   □ Gummy   □ Sticky   □ Chewy

5. Flavor & Finish

Flavor Intensity: □ DOA   □ Subtle   □ Bold

Flavor Profile: [Very sweet] 1   2   3   4   5   6   7   8   9   10 [Very bitter]

□ sweet   □ sour   □ bitter   □ salty   □ umami/savory

Flavors: _____

_____

Finish: □ Fades quickly   □ Lingers pleasantly   □ Won't go away

Recommend for: _____

Notes: _____

_____

Eat it again?   □ Can't pay me to   □ Maybe   □ Sure   □ Yes, please!

Rating: ☆ ☆ ☆ ☆ ☆

Chocolate Savoring Notes

DATE, OCCASION: _____ COMPANION(S): _____

CHOCOLATIER: _____ LOCATION: _____

CHOCOLATE NAME: _____

CACAO ORIGIN: _____ Cacao _____%

TYPE: ☐ Dark ☐ Semi-Sweet ☐ Milk ☐ White

☐ Specialty Flavor: _____

Category: _____ (Bar, truffle, etc.)

Key Ingredients: _____

Allergy status. Contains: ☐ Gluten / Wheat ☐ Milk

☐ Soy ☐ Eggs

☐ Peanuts ☐ Tree Nuts

☐ Corn ☐ Sesame

☐ other: _____

Certifications: ☐ Fair-Trade ☐Rainforest Alliance

☐ USDA Organic ☐ Non-GMO Project

☐ Gluten-Free ☐ Kosher

☐ Vegan ☐ Paleo

Price: _____ Available at: _____

Label / Graphics: _____

_____

1. Appearance

Color: □ Charcoal Brown □ Mocha □ Caramel □ Ivory

Surface: □ Cloudy □ Smooth □ Shiny / Glossy □ Dull

□ Molted □ Waxy □ Discolored □ Bubbles

□ Even color □ Fine grain □ Coarse □ Crumbly □ Stratified

2. The Snap – the sound.

Breaks: □ Sharply (cracking) □ Loudly □ Quietly □ Softly

3. Aroma – the smell.

□ Roasted: _____ □ Nutty: _____ □ Caramel: _____

□ Dairy: _____ □ Vanilla: _____ □ Fruity: _____

□ Vegetal: _____ □ Spice: _____ □ Floral: _____

4. Texture – Mouthfeel.

Melts: □ Quickly □ Slowly

Feels: □ Smooth □ Creamy □ Greasy □ Slimy

□ Hard □ Waxy □ Graining □ Gritty □ Powdery

Texture: □ Cakelike □ Fudgy □ Gummy □ Sticky □ Chewy

5. Flavor & Finish

Flavor Intensity: □ DOA □ Subtle □ Bold

Flavor Profile: [Very sweet] 1　2　3　4　5　6　7　8　9　10 [Very bitter]

□ sweet □ sour □ bitter □ salty □ umami/savory

Flavors: _____

_____

Finish: □ Fades quickly □ Lingers pleasantly □ Won't go away

Recommend for: _____

Notes: _____

_____

Eat it again? □ Can't pay me to □ Maybe □ Sure □ Yes, please!

Rating: ☆ ☆ ☆ ☆ ☆

Chocolate Savoring Notes

DATE, OCCASION: _____   COMPANION(S): _____

CHOCOLATIER: _____   LOCATION: _____

CHOCOLATE NAME: _____

CACAO ORIGIN: _____   Cacao _____%

TYPE: □ Dark   □ Semi-Sweet   □ Milk   □ White

            □ Specialty Flavor: _____

Category: _____ (Bar, truffle, etc.)

Key Ingredients: _____

Allergy status. Contains: □ Gluten / Wheat   □ Milk

                             □ Soy   □ Eggs

                             □ Peanuts   □ Tree Nuts

                             □ Corn   □ Sesame

                             □ other: _____

Certifications: □ Fair-Trade   □ Rainforest Alliance

                             □ USDA Organic   □ Non-GMO Project

                             □ Gluten-Free   □ Kosher

                             □ Vegan   □ Paleo

Price: _____   Available at: _____

Label / Graphics: _____

_____

1. Appearance

Color: □ Charcoal Brown □ Mocha □ Caramel □ Ivory

Surface: □ Cloudy □ Smooth □ Shiny / Glossy □ Dull

□ Molted □ Waxy □ Discolored □ Bubbles

□ Even color □ Fine grain □ Coarse □ Crumbly □ Stratified

2. The Snap – the sound.

Breaks: □ Sharply (cracking) □ Loudly □ Quietly □ Softly

3. Aroma – the smell.

□ Roasted: _____ □ Nutty: _____ □ Caramel: _____

□ Dairy: _____ □ Vanilla: _____ □ Fruity: _____

□ Vegetal: _____ □ Spice: _____ □ Floral: _____

4. Texture – Mouthfeel.

Melts: □ Quickly □ Slowly

Feels: □ Smooth □ Creamy □ Greasy □ Slimy

□ Hard □ Waxy □ Graining □ Gritty □ Powdery

Texture: □ Cakelike □ Fudgy □ Gummy □ Sticky □ Chewy

5. Flavor & Finish

Flavor Intensity: □ DOA □ Subtle □ Bold

Flavor Profile: [Very sweet] 1 2 3 4 5 6 7 8 9 10 [Very bitter]

□ sweet □ sour □ bitter □ salty □ umami/savory

Flavors: _____

_____

Finish: □ Fades quickly □ Lingers pleasantly □ Won't go away

Recommend for: _____

Notes: _____

_____

Eat it again? □ Can't pay me to □ Maybe □ Sure □ Yes, please!

Rating: ☆ ☆ ☆ ☆ ☆

Chocolate Savoring Notes

DATE, OCCASION: _____   COMPANION(S): _____

CHOCOLATIER: _____   LOCATION: _____

CHOCOLATE NAME: _____

CACAO ORIGIN: _____   Cacao _____%

TYPE: □ Dark   □ Semi-Sweet   □ Milk   □ White

□ Specialty Flavor: _____

Category: _____ (Bar, truffle, etc.)

Key Ingredients: _____

Allergy status. Contains: □ Gluten / Wheat   □ Milk

□ Soy   □ Eggs

□ Peanuts   □ Tree Nuts

□ Corn   □ Sesame

□ other: _____

Certifications: □ Fair-Trade   □ Rainforest Alliance

□ USDA Organic   □ Non-GMO Project

□ Gluten-Free   □ Kosher

□ Vegan   □ Paleo

Price: _____   Available at: _____

Label / Graphics: _____

_____

1. Appearance

Color: □ Charcoal Brown □ Mocha □ Caramel □ Ivory

Surface: □ Cloudy □ Smooth □ Shiny / Glossy □ Dull

□ Molted □ Waxy □ Discolored □ Bubbles

□ Even color □ Fine grain □ Coarse □ Crumbly □ Stratified

2. The Snap – the sound.

Breaks: □ Sharply (cracking) □ Loudly □ Quietly □ Softly

3. Aroma – the smell.

□ Roasted: _____ □ Nutty: _____ □ Caramel: _____

□ Dairy: _____ □ Vanilla: _____ □ Fruity: _____

□ Vegetal: _____ □ Spice: _____ □ Floral: _____

4. Texture – Mouthfeel.

Melts: □ Quickly □ Slowly

Feels: □ Smooth □ Creamy □ Greasy □ Slimy

□ Hard □ Waxy □ Graining □ Gritty □ Powdery

Texture: □ Cakelike □ Fudgy □ Gummy □ Sticky □ Chewy

5. Flavor & Finish

Flavor Intensity: □ DOA □ Subtle □ Bold

Flavor Profile: [Very sweet] 1 2 3 4 5 6 7 8 9 10 [Very bitter]

□ sweet □ sour □ bitter □ salty □ umami/savory

Flavors: _____

_____

Finish: □ Fades quickly □ Lingers pleasantly □ Won't go away

Recommend for: _____

Notes: _____

_____

Eat it again? □ Can't pay me to □ Maybe □ Sure □ Yes, please!

Rating: ☆ ☆ ☆ ☆ ☆

Chocolate Savoring Notes

DATE, OCCASION: _____   COMPANION(S): _____

CHOCOLATIER: _____   LOCATION: _____

CHOCOLATE NAME: _____

CACAO ORIGIN: _____   Cacao _____%

TYPE: □ Dark   □ Semi-Sweet   □ Milk   □ White

              □ Specialty Flavor: _____

Category: _____ (Bar, truffle, etc.)

Key Ingredients: _____

Allergy status. Contains: □ Gluten / Wheat   □ Milk

                              □ Soy   □ Eggs

                              □ Peanuts   □ Tree Nuts

                              □ Corn   □ Sesame

                              □ other: _____

Certifications: □ Fair-Trade   □ Rainforest Alliance

                    □ USDA Organic   □ Non-GMO Project

                    □ Gluten-Free   □ Kosher

                    □ Vegan   □ Paleo

Price: _____   Available at: _____

Label / Graphics: _____

_____

1. Appearance

Color: ☐ Charcoal Brown ☐ Mocha ☐ Caramel ☐ Ivory

Surface: ☐ Cloudy ☐ Smooth ☐ Shiny / Glossy ☐ Dull

☐ Molted ☐ Waxy ☐ Discolored ☐ Bubbles

☐ Even color ☐ Fine grain ☐ Coarse ☐ Crumbly ☐ Stratified

2. The Snap – the sound.

Breaks: ☐ Sharply (cracking) ☐ Loudly ☐ Quietly ☐ Softly

3. Aroma – the smell.

☐ Roasted: _____ ☐ Nutty: _____ ☐ Caramel: _____

☐ Dairy: _____ ☐ Vanilla: _____ ☐ Fruity: _____

☐ Vegetal: _____ ☐ Spice: _____ ☐ Floral: _____

4. Texture – Mouthfeel.

Melts: ☐ Quickly ☐ Slowly

Feels: ☐ Smooth ☐ Creamy ☐ Greasy ☐ Slimy

☐ Hard ☐ Waxy ☐ Graining ☐ Gritty ☐ Powdery

Texture: ☐ Cakelike ☐ Fudgy ☐ Gummy ☐ Sticky ☐ Chewy

5. Flavor & Finish

Flavor Intensity: ☐ DOA ☐ Subtle ☐ Bold

Flavor Profile: [Very sweet] 1 2 3 4 5 6 7 8 9 10 [Very bitter]

☐ sweet ☐ sour ☐ bitter ☐ salty ☐ umami/savory

Flavors: _____

_____

Finish: ☐ Fades quickly ☐ Lingers pleasantly ☐ Won't go away

Recommend for: _____

Notes: _____

_____

Eat it again? ☐ Can't pay me to ☐ Maybe ☐ Sure ☐ Yes, please!

Rating: ☆ ☆ ☆ ☆ ☆

Chocolate Savoring Notes

DATE, OCCASION: _____   COMPANION(S): _____

CHOCOLATIER: _____   LOCATION: _____

CHOCOLATE NAME: _____

CACAO ORIGIN: _____   Cacao _____%

TYPE: □ Dark   □ Semi-Sweet   □ Milk   □ White

□ Specialty Flavor: _____

Category: _____ (Bar, truffle, etc.)

Key Ingredients: _____

Allergy status. Contains: □ Gluten / Wheat   □ Milk

□ Soy   □ Eggs

□ Peanuts   □ Tree Nuts

□ Corn   □ Sesame

□ other: _____

Certifications: □ Fair-Trade   □ Rainforest Alliance

□ USDA Organic   □ Non-GMO Project

□ Gluten-Free   □ Kosher

□ Vegan   □ Paleo

Price: _____   Available at: _____

Label / Graphics: _____

_____

1. Appearance

Color: □ Charcoal Brown   □ Mocha   □ Caramel   □ Ivory

Surface: □ Cloudy   □ Smooth   □ Shiny / Glossy   □ Dull

           □ Molted   □ Waxy   □ Discolored   □ Bubbles

           □ Even color   □ Fine grain   □ Coarse   □ Crumbly   □ Stratified

2. The Snap – the sound.

Breaks: □ Sharply (cracking)   □ Loudly   □ Quietly   □ Softly

3. Aroma – the smell.

□ Roasted: _____   □ Nutty: _____   □ Caramel: _____

□ Dairy: _____   □ Vanilla: _____   □ Fruity: _____

□ Vegetal: _____   □ Spice: _____   □ Floral: _____

4. Texture – Mouthfeel.

Melts: □ Quickly   □ Slowly

Feels: □ Smooth   □ Creamy   □ Greasy   □ Slimy

        □ Hard   □ Waxy   □ Graining   □ Gritty   □ Powdery

Texture: □ Cakelike   □ Fudgy   □ Gummy   □ Sticky   □ Chewy

5. Flavor & Finish

Flavor Intensity: □ DOA   □ Subtle   □ Bold

Flavor Profile: [Very sweet] 1   2   3   4   5   6   7   8   9   10 [Very bitter]

                    □ sweet   □ sour   □ bitter   □ salty   □ umami/savory

Flavors: _____

_____

Finish: □ Fades quickly   □ Lingers pleasantly   □ Won't go away

Recommend for: _____

Notes: _____

_____

Eat it again?   □ Can't pay me to   □ Maybe   □ Sure   □ Yes, please!

Rating: ☆ ☆ ☆ ☆ ☆

Chocolate Savoring Notes

DATE, OCCASION: _____ COMPANION(S): _____

CHOCOLATIER: _____ LOCATION: _____

CHOCOLATE NAME: _____

CACAO ORIGIN: _____ Cacao _____%

TYPE: □ Dark   □ Semi-Sweet   □ Milk   □ White

          □ Specialty Flavor: _____

Category: _____ (Bar, truffle, etc.)

Key Ingredients: _____

Allergy status. Contains: □ Gluten / Wheat   □ Milk

                           □ Soy   □ Eggs

                           □ Peanuts   □ Tree Nuts

                           □ Corn   □ Sesame

                           □ other: _____

Certifications: □ Fair-Trade   □Rainforest Alliance

                           □ USDA Organic   □ Non-GMO Project

                           □ Gluten-Free   □ Kosher

                           □ Vegan   □ Paleo

Price: _____   Available at: _____

Label / Graphics: _____

_____

1. Appearance

Color: □ Charcoal Brown □ Mocha □ Caramel □ Ivory

Surface: □ Cloudy □ Smooth □ Shiny / Glossy □ Dull

□ Molted □ Waxy □ Discolored □ Bubbles

□ Even color □ Fine grain □ Coarse □ Crumbly □ Stratified

2. The Snap – the sound.

Breaks: □ Sharply (cracking) □ Loudly □ Quietly □ Softly

3. Aroma – the smell.

□ Roasted: _____ □ Nutty: _____ □ Caramel: _____

□ Dairy: _____ □ Vanilla: _____ □ Fruity: _____

□ Vegetal: _____ □ Spice: _____ □ Floral: _____

4. Texture – Mouthfeel.

Melts: □ Quickly □ Slowly

Feels: □ Smooth □ Creamy □ Greasy □ Slimy

□ Hard □ Waxy □ Graining □ Gritty □ Powdery

Texture: □ Cakelike □ Fudgy □ Gummy □ Sticky □ Chewy

5. Flavor & Finish

Flavor Intensity: □ DOA □ Subtle □ Bold

Flavor Profile: [Very sweet] 1 2 3 4 5 6 7 8 9 10 [Very bitter]

□ sweet □ sour □ bitter □ salty □ umami/savory

Flavors: _____

_____

Finish: □ Fades quickly □ Lingers pleasantly □ Won't go away

Recommend for: _____

Notes: _____

_____

Eat it again? □ Can't pay me to □ Maybe □ Sure □ Yes, please!

Rating: ☆ ☆ ☆ ☆ ☆

Chocolate Savoring Notes

DATE, OCCASION: _____   COMPANION(S): _____

CHOCOLATIER: _____   LOCATION: _____

CHOCOLATE NAME: _____

CACAO ORIGIN: _____   Cacao _____%

TYPE: □ Dark   □ Semi-Sweet   □ Milk   □ White

           □ Specialty Flavor: _____

Category: _____ (Bar, truffle, etc.)

Key Ingredients: _____

Allergy status. Contains: □ Gluten / Wheat   □ Milk

                            □ Soy   □ Eggs

                            □ Peanuts   □ Tree Nuts

                            □ Corn   □ Sesame

                            □ other: _____

Certifications: □ Fair-Trade   □ Rainforest Alliance

                            □ USDA Organic   □ Non-GMO Project

                            □ Gluten-Free   □ Kosher

                            □ Vegan   □ Paleo

Price: _____   Available at: _____

Label / Graphics: _____

_____

1. Appearance

Color: ☐ Charcoal Brown ☐ Mocha ☐ Caramel ☐ Ivory

Surface: ☐ Cloudy ☐ Smooth ☐ Shiny / Glossy ☐ Dull

☐ Molted ☐ Waxy ☐ Discolored ☐ Bubbles

☐ Even color ☐ Fine grain ☐ Coarse ☐ Crumbly ☐ Stratified

2. The Snap – the sound.

Breaks: ☐ Sharply (cracking) ☐ Loudly ☐ Quietly ☐ Softly

3. Aroma – the smell.

☐ Roasted: _____ ☐ Nutty: _____ ☐ Caramel: _____

☐ Dairy: _____ ☐ Vanilla: _____ ☐ Fruity: _____

☐ Vegetal: _____ ☐ Spice: _____ ☐ Floral: _____

4. Texture – Mouthfeel.

Melts: ☐ Quickly ☐ Slowly

Feels: ☐ Smooth ☐ Creamy ☐ Greasy ☐ Slimy

☐ Hard ☐ Waxy ☐ Graining ☐ Gritty ☐ Powdery

Texture: ☐ Cakelike ☐ Fudgy ☐ Gummy ☐ Sticky ☐ Chewy

5. Flavor & Finish

Flavor Intensity: ☐ DOA ☐ Subtle ☐ Bold

Flavor Profile: [Very sweet] 1   2   3   4   5   6   7   8   9   10 [Very bitter]

☐ sweet ☐ sour ☐ bitter ☐ salty ☐ umami/savory

Flavors: _____

_____

Finish: ☐ Fades quickly ☐ Lingers pleasantly ☐ Won't go away

Recommend for: _____

Notes: _____

_____

Eat it again? ☐ Can't pay me to ☐ Maybe ☐ Sure ☐ Yes, please!

Rating: ☆ ☆ ☆ ☆ ☆

Chocolate Savoring Notes

DATE, OCCASION: _____   COMPANION(S): _____

CHOCOLATIER: _____   LOCATION: _____

CHOCOLATE NAME: _____

CACAO ORIGIN: _____   Cacao _____%

TYPE: □ Dark   □ Semi-Sweet   □ Milk   □ White

□ Specialty Flavor: _____

Category: _____ (Bar, truffle, etc.)

Key Ingredients: _____

Allergy status. Contains: □ Gluten / Wheat   □ Milk

□ Soy   □ Eggs

□ Peanuts   □ Tree Nuts

□ Corn   □ Sesame

□ other: _____

Certifications: □ Fair-Trade   □ Rainforest Alliance

□ USDA Organic   □ Non-GMO Project

□ Gluten-Free   □ Kosher

□ Vegan   □ Paleo

Price: _____   Available at: _____

Label / Graphics: _____

_____

1. Appearance

Color: □ Charcoal Brown □ Mocha □ Caramel □ Ivory

Surface: □ Cloudy □ Smooth □ Shiny / Glossy □ Dull

□ Molted □ Waxy □ Discolored □ Bubbles

□ Even color □ Fine grain □ Coarse □ Crumbly □ Stratified

2. The Snap – the sound.

Breaks: □ Sharply (cracking) □ Loudly □ Quietly □ Softly

3. Aroma – the smell.

□ Roasted: _____ □ Nutty: _____ □ Caramel: _____

□ Dairy: _____ □ Vanilla: _____ □ Fruity: _____

□ Vegetal: _____ □ Spice: _____ □ Floral: _____

4. Texture – Mouthfeel.

Melts: □ Quickly □ Slowly

Feels: □ Smooth □ Creamy □ Greasy □ Slimy

□ Hard □ Waxy □ Graining □ Gritty □ Powdery

Texture: □ Cakelike □ Fudgy □ Gummy □ Sticky □ Chewy

5. Flavor & Finish

Flavor Intensity: □ DOA □ Subtle □ Bold

Flavor Profile: [Very sweet] 1 2 3 4 5 6 7 8 9 10 [Very bitter]

□ sweet □ sour □ bitter □ salty □ umami/savory

Flavors: _____

_____

Finish: □ Fades quickly □ Lingers pleasantly □ Won't go away

Recommend for: _____

Notes: _____

_____

Eat it again? □ Can't pay me to □ Maybe □ Sure □ Yes, please!

Rating: ☆ ☆ ☆ ☆ ☆

Chocolate Savoring Notes

DATE, OCCASION: _____   COMPANION(S):_____

CHOCOLATIER: _____   LOCATION: _____

CHOCOLATE NAME: _____

CACAO ORIGIN: _____   Cacao _____%

TYPE: ☐ Dark   ☐ Semi-Sweet   ☐ Milk   ☐ White

☐ Specialty Flavor: _____

Category: _____ (Bar, truffle, etc.)

Key Ingredients: _____

Allergy status. Contains: ☐ Gluten / Wheat   ☐ Milk

☐ Soy   ☐ Eggs

☐ Peanuts   ☐ Tree Nuts

☐ Corn   ☐ Sesame

☐ other: _____

Certifications: ☐ Fair-Trade   ☐ Rainforest Alliance

☐ USDA Organic   ☐ Non-GMO Project

☐ Gluten-Free   ☐ Kosher

☐ Vegan   ☐ Paleo

Price: _____   Available at: _____

Label / Graphics: _____

_____

1. Appearance

Color: □ Charcoal Brown   □ Mocha   □ Caramel   □ Ivory

Surface: □ Cloudy   □ Smooth   □ Shiny / Glossy   □ Dull

□ Molted   □ Waxy   □ Discolored   □ Bubbles

□ Even color   □ Fine grain   □ Coarse   □ Crumbly   □ Stratified

2. The Snap – the sound.

Breaks: □ Sharply (cracking)   □ Loudly   □ Quietly   □ Softly

3. Aroma – the smell.

□ Roasted: _____   □ Nutty: _____   □ Caramel: _____

□ Dairy: _____   □ Vanilla: _____   □ Fruity: _____

□ Vegetal: _____   □ Spice: _____   □ Floral: _____

4. Texture – Mouthfeel.

Melts: □ Quickly   □ Slowly

Feels: □ Smooth   □ Creamy   □ Greasy   □ Slimy

□ Hard   □ Waxy   □ Graining   □ Gritty   □ Powdery

Texture: □ Cakelike   □ Fudgy   □ Gummy   □ Sticky   □ Chewy

5. Flavor & Finish

Flavor Intensity: □ DOA   □ Subtle   □ Bold

Flavor Profile: [Very sweet] 1   2   3   4   5   6   7   8   9   10 [Very bitter]

□ sweet   □ sour   □ bitter   □ salty   □ umami/savory

Flavors: _____

_____

Finish: □ Fades quickly   □ Lingers pleasantly   □ Won't go away

Recommend for: _____

Notes: _____

_____

Eat it again?   □ Can't pay me to   □ Maybe   □ Sure   □ Yes, please!

Rating: ☆ ☆ ☆ ☆ ☆

Chocolate Savoring Notes

DATE, OCCASION: _____ COMPANION(S): _____

CHOCOLATIER: _____ LOCATION: _____

CHOCOLATE NAME: _____

CACAO ORIGIN: _____ Cacao _____%

TYPE: □ Dark   □ Semi-Sweet   □ Milk   □ White

             □ Specialty Flavor: _____

Category: _____ (Bar, truffle, etc.)

Key Ingredients: _____

Allergy status. Contains: □ Gluten / Wheat   □ Milk

                            □ Soy   □ Eggs

                            □ Peanuts   □ Tree Nuts

                            □ Corn   □ Sesame

                            □ other: _____

Certifications: □ Fair-Trade   □Rainforest Alliance

                  □ USDA Organic   □ Non-GMO Project

                  □ Gluten-Free   □ Kosher

                  □ Vegan   □ Paleo

Price: _____   Available at: _____

Label / Graphics: _____

_____

1. Appearance

Color: □ Charcoal Brown □ Mocha □ Caramel □ Ivory

Surface: □ Cloudy □ Smooth □ Shiny / Glossy □ Dull

□ Molted □ Waxy □ Discolored □ Bubbles

□ Even color □ Fine grain □ Coarse □ Crumbly □ Stratified

2. The Snap – the sound.

Breaks: □ Sharply (cracking) □ Loudly □ Quietly □ Softly

3. Aroma – the smell.

□ Roasted: _____ □ Nutty: _____ □ Caramel: _____

□ Dairy: _____ □ Vanilla: _____ □ Fruity: _____

□ Vegetal: _____ □ Spice: _____ □ Floral: _____

4. Texture – Mouthfeel.

Melts: □ Quickly □ Slowly

Feels: □ Smooth □ Creamy □ Greasy □ Slimy

□ Hard □ Waxy □ Graining □ Gritty □ Powdery

Texture: □ Cakelike □ Fudgy □ Gummy □ Sticky □ Chewy

5. Flavor & Finish

Flavor Intensity: □ DOA □ Subtle □ Bold

Flavor Profile: [Very sweet] 1 2 3 4 5 6 7 8 9 10 [Very bitter]

□ sweet □ sour □ bitter □ salty □ umami/savory

Flavors: _____

_____

Finish: □ Fades quickly □ Lingers pleasantly □ Won't go away

Recommend for: _____

Notes: _____

_____

Eat it again? □ Can't pay me to □ Maybe □ Sure □ Yes, please!

Rating: ☆ ☆ ☆ ☆ ☆

Chocolate Savoring Notes

DATE, OCCASION: _____   COMPANION(S): _____

CHOCOLATIER: _____   LOCATION: _____

CHOCOLATE NAME: _____

CACAO ORIGIN: _____   Cacao _____%

TYPE: □ Dark   □ Semi-Sweet   □ Milk   □ White

          □ Specialty Flavor: _____

Category: _____ (Bar, truffle, etc.)

Key Ingredients: _____

Allergy status. Contains: □ Gluten / Wheat   □ Milk

                                 □ Soy   □ Eggs

                                 □ Peanuts   □ Tree Nuts

                                 □ Corn   □ Sesame

                                 □ other: _____

Certifications: □ Fair-Trade   □ Rainforest Alliance

                        □ USDA Organic   □ Non-GMO Project

                        □ Gluten-Free   □ Kosher

                        □ Vegan   □ Paleo

Price: _____   Available at: _____

Label / Graphics: _____

_____

1. Appearance

Color: ☐ Charcoal Brown ☐ Mocha ☐ Caramel ☐ Ivory

Surface: ☐ Cloudy ☐ Smooth ☐ Shiny / Glossy ☐ Dull

☐ Molted ☐ Waxy ☐ Discolored ☐ Bubbles

☐ Even color ☐ Fine grain ☐ Coarse ☐ Crumbly ☐ Stratified

2. The Snap – the sound.

Breaks: ☐ Sharply (cracking) ☐ Loudly ☐ Quietly ☐ Softly

3. Aroma – the smell.

☐ Roasted: _____ ☐ Nutty: _____ ☐ Caramel: _____

☐ Dairy: _____ ☐ Vanilla: _____ ☐ Fruity: _____

☐ Vegetal: _____ ☐ Spice: _____ ☐ Floral: _____

4. Texture – Mouthfeel.

Melts: ☐ Quickly ☐ Slowly

Feels: ☐ Smooth ☐ Creamy ☐ Greasy ☐ Slimy

☐ Hard ☐ Waxy ☐ Graining ☐ Gritty ☐ Powdery

Texture: ☐ Cakelike ☐ Fudgy ☐ Gummy ☐ Sticky ☐ Chewy

5. Flavor & Finish

Flavor Intensity: ☐ DOA ☐ Subtle ☐ Bold

Flavor Profile: [Very sweet] 1   2   3   4   5   6   7   8   9   10 [Very bitter]

☐ sweet ☐ sour ☐ bitter ☐ salty ☐ umami/savory

Flavors: _____

_____

Finish: ☐ Fades quickly ☐ Lingers pleasantly ☐ Won't go away

Recommend for: _____

Notes: _____

_____

Eat it again? ☐ Can't pay me to ☐ Maybe ☐ Sure ☐ Yes, please!

Rating: ☆ ☆ ☆ ☆ ☆

Chocolate Savoring Notes

DATE, OCCASION: _____ COMPANION(S):_____

CHOCOLATIER: _____ LOCATION: _____

CHOCOLATE NAME: _____

CACAO ORIGIN: _____ Cacao _____%

TYPE: □ Dark   □ Semi-Sweet   □ Milk   □ White

          □ Specialty Flavor: _____

Category: _____ (Bar, truffle, etc.)

Key Ingredients: _____

Allergy status. Contains: □ Gluten / Wheat   □ Milk

                            □ Soy   □ Eggs

                            □ Peanuts   □ Tree Nuts

                            □ Corn   □ Sesame

                            □ other: _____

Certifications: □ Fair-Trade   □ Rainforest Alliance

                    □ USDA Organic   □ Non-GMO Project

                    □ Gluten-Free   □ Kosher

                    □ Vegan   □ Paleo

Price: _____   Available at: _____

Label / Graphics: _____

_____

1. Appearance

Color: □ Charcoal Brown   □ Mocha   □ Caramel   □ Ivory

Surface: □ Cloudy   □ Smooth   □ Shiny / Glossy   □ Dull

□ Molted   □ Waxy   □ Discolored   □ Bubbles

□ Even color   □ Fine grain   □ Coarse   □ Crumbly   □ Stratified

2. The Snap – the sound.

Breaks: □ Sharply (cracking)   □ Loudly   □ Quietly   □ Softly

3. Aroma – the smell.

□ Roasted: _____   □ Nutty: _____   □ Caramel: _____

□ Dairy: _____   □ Vanilla: _____   □ Fruity: _____

□ Vegetal: _____   □ Spice: _____   □ Floral: _____

4. Texture – Mouthfeel.

Melts: □ Quickly   □ Slowly

Feels: □ Smooth   □ Creamy   □ Greasy   □ Slimy

□ Hard   □ Waxy   □ Graining   □ Gritty   □ Powdery

Texture: □ Cakelike   □ Fudgy   □ Gummy   □ Sticky   □ Chewy

5. Flavor & Finish

Flavor Intensity: □ DOA   □ Subtle   □ Bold

Flavor Profile: [Very sweet] 1   2   3   4   5   6   7   8   9   10 [Very bitter]

□ sweet   □ sour   □ bitter   □ salty   □ umami/savory

Flavors: _____

_____

Finish: □ Fades quickly   □ Lingers pleasantly   □ Won't go away

Recommend for: _____

Notes: _____

_____

Eat it again?   □ Can't pay me to   □ Maybe   □Sure   □ Yes, please!

Rating: ☆ ☆ ☆ ☆ ☆

Chocolate Savoring Notes

DATE, OCCASION: _____   COMPANION(S): _____

CHOCOLATIER: _____   LOCATION: _____

CHOCOLATE NAME: _____

CACAO ORIGIN: _____   Cacao _____%

TYPE: □ Dark   □ Semi-Sweet   □ Milk   □ White

            □ Specialty Flavor: _____

Category: _____ (Bar, truffle, etc.)

Key Ingredients: _____

Allergy status. Contains: □ Gluten / Wheat   □ Milk

                                  □ Soy   □ Eggs

                                  □ Peanuts   □ Tree Nuts

                                  □ Corn   □ Sesame

                                  □ other: _____

Certifications: □ Fair-Trade   □Rainforest Alliance

                         □ USDA Organic   □ Non-GMO Project

                         □ Gluten-Free   □ Kosher

                         □ Vegan   □ Paleo

Price: _____   Available at: _____

Label / Graphics: _____

_____

1. Appearance

Color: □ Charcoal Brown   □ Mocha   □ Caramel   □ Ivory

Surface: □ Cloudy   □ Smooth   □ Shiny / Glossy   □ Dull

□ Molted   □ Waxy   □ Discolored   □ Bubbles

□ Even color   □ Fine grain   □ Coarse   □ Crumbly   □ Stratified

2. The Snap – the sound.

Breaks: □ Sharply (cracking)   □ Loudly   □ Quietly   □ Softly

3. Aroma – the smell.

□ Roasted: _____   □ Nutty: _____   □ Caramel: _____

□ Dairy: _____   □ Vanilla: _____   □ Fruity: _____

□ Vegetal: _____   □ Spice: _____   □ Floral: _____

4. Texture – Mouthfeel.

Melts: □ Quickly   □ Slowly

Feels: □ Smooth   □ Creamy   □ Greasy   □ Slimy

□ Hard   □ Waxy   □ Graining   □ Gritty   □ Powdery

Texture: □ Cakelike   □ Fudgy   □ Gummy   □ Sticky   □ Chewy

5. Flavor & Finish

Flavor Intensity: □ DOA   □ Subtle   □ Bold

Flavor Profile: [Very sweet] 1   2   3   4   5   6   7   8   9   10 [Very bitter]

□ sweet   □ sour   □ bitter   □ salty   □ umami/savory

Flavors: _____

_____

Finish: □ Fades quickly   □ Lingers pleasantly   □ Won't go away

Recommend for: _____

Notes: _____

_____

Eat it again?   □ Can't pay me to   □ Maybe   □ Sure   □ Yes, please!

Rating: ☆ ☆ ☆ ☆ ☆

Chocolate Savoring Notes

DATE, OCCASION: _____   COMPANION(S): _____

CHOCOLATIER: _____   LOCATION: _____

CHOCOLATE NAME: _____

CACAO ORIGIN: _____   Cacao _____%

TYPE: □ Dark   □ Semi-Sweet   □ Milk   □ White

□ Specialty Flavor: _____

Category: _____ (Bar, truffle, etc.)

Key Ingredients: _____

Allergy status. Contains: □ Gluten / Wheat   □ Milk

□ Soy   □ Eggs

□ Peanuts   □ Tree Nuts

□ Corn   □ Sesame

□ other: _____

Certifications: □ Fair-Trade   □ Rainforest Alliance

□ USDA Organic   □ Non-GMO Project

□ Gluten-Free   □ Kosher

□ Vegan   □ Paleo

Price: _____   Available at: _____

Label / Graphics: _____

_____

1. Appearance

Color: □ Charcoal Brown □ Mocha □ Caramel □ Ivory

Surface: □ Cloudy □ Smooth □ Shiny / Glossy □ Dull

□ Molted □ Waxy □ Discolored □ Bubbles

□ Even color □ Fine grain □ Coarse □ Crumbly □ Stratified

2. The Snap – the sound.

Breaks: □ Sharply (cracking) □ Loudly □ Quietly □ Softly

3. Aroma – the smell.

□ Roasted: _____ □ Nutty: _____ □ Caramel: _____

□ Dairy: _____ □ Vanilla: _____ □ Fruity: _____

□ Vegetal: _____ □ Spice: _____ □ Floral: _____

4. Texture – Mouthfeel.

Melts: □ Quickly □ Slowly

Feels: □ Smooth □ Creamy □ Greasy □ Slimy

□ Hard □ Waxy □ Graining □ Gritty □ Powdery

Texture: □ Cakelike □ Fudgy □ Gummy □ Sticky □ Chewy

5. Flavor & Finish

Flavor Intensity: □ DOA □ Subtle □ Bold

Flavor Profile: [Very sweet] 1   2   3   4   5   6   7   8   9   10 [Very bitter]

□ sweet □ sour □ bitter □ salty □ umami/savory

Flavors: _____

_____

Finish: □ Fades quickly □ Lingers pleasantly □ Won't go away

Recommend for: _____

Notes: _____

_____

Eat it again? □ Can't pay me to □ Maybe □ Sure □ Yes, please!

Rating: ☆ ☆ ☆ ☆ ☆

Chocolate Savoring Notes

DATE, OCCASION: _____   COMPANION(S): _____

CHOCOLATIER: _____   LOCATION: _____

CHOCOLATE NAME: _____

CACAO ORIGIN: _____   Cacao _____%

TYPE: □ Dark   □ Semi-Sweet   □ Milk   □ White

□ Specialty Flavor: _____

Category: _____ (Bar, truffle, etc.)

Key Ingredients: _____

Allergy status. Contains: □ Gluten / Wheat   □ Milk

□ Soy   □ Eggs

□ Peanuts   □ Tree Nuts

□ Corn   □ Sesame

□ other: _____

Certifications: □ Fair-Trade   □ Rainforest Alliance

□ USDA Organic   □ Non-GMO Project

□ Gluten-Free   □ Kosher

□ Vegan   □ Paleo

Price: _____   Available at: _____

Label / Graphics: _____

_____

1. Appearance

Color: ☐ Charcoal Brown   ☐ Mocha   ☐ Caramel   ☐ Ivory

Surface: ☐ Cloudy   ☐ Smooth   ☐ Shiny / Glossy   ☐ Dull

           ☐ Molted   ☐ Waxy   ☐ Discolored   ☐ Bubbles

           ☐ Even color   ☐ Fine grain   ☐ Coarse   ☐ Crumbly   ☐ Stratified

2. The Snap – the sound.

Breaks: ☐ Sharply (cracking)   ☐ Loudly   ☐ Quietly   ☐ Softly

3. Aroma – the smell.

☐ Roasted: _____   ☐ Nutty: _____   ☐ Caramel: _____

☐ Dairy: _____   ☐ Vanilla: _____   ☐ Fruity: _____

☐ Vegetal: _____   ☐ Spice: _____   ☐ Floral: _____

4. Texture – Mouthfeel.

Melts: ☐ Quickly   ☐ Slowly

Feels: ☐ Smooth   ☐ Creamy   ☐ Greasy   ☐ Slimy

          ☐ Hard   ☐ Waxy   ☐ Graining   ☐ Gritty   ☐ Powdery

Texture: ☐ Cakelike   ☐ Fudgy   ☐ Gummy   ☐ Sticky   ☐ Chewy

5. Flavor & Finish

Flavor Intensity: ☐ DOA   ☐ Subtle   ☐ Bold

Flavor Profile: [Very sweet] 1   2   3   4   5   6   7   8   9   10 [Very bitter]

                          ☐ sweet   ☐ sour   ☐ bitter   ☐ salty   ☐ umami/savory

Flavors: _____

_____

Finish: ☐ Fades quickly   ☐ Lingers pleasantly   ☐ Won't go away

Recommend for: _____

Notes: _____

_____

Eat it again?   ☐ Can't pay me to   ☐ Maybe   ☐ Sure   ☐ Yes, please!

Rating: ☆ ☆ ☆ ☆ ☆

Chocolate Savoring Notes

DATE, OCCASION: _____   COMPANION(S): _____

CHOCOLATIER: _____   LOCATION: _____

CHOCOLATE NAME: _____

CACAO ORIGIN: _____   Cacao _____%

TYPE: □ Dark   □ Semi-Sweet   □ Milk   □ White

□ Specialty Flavor: _____

Category: _____ (Bar, truffle, etc.)

Key Ingredients: _____

Allergy status. Contains: □ Gluten / Wheat   □ Milk

□ Soy   □ Eggs

□ Peanuts   □ Tree Nuts

□ Corn   □ Sesame

□ other: _____

Certifications: □ Fair-Trade   □ Rainforest Alliance

□ USDA Organic   □ Non-GMO Project

□ Gluten-Free   □ Kosher

□ Vegan   □ Paleo

Price: _____   Available at: _____

Label / Graphics: _____

_____

1. Appearance

Color: ☐ Charcoal Brown ☐ Mocha ☐ Caramel ☐ Ivory

Surface: ☐ Cloudy ☐ Smooth ☐ Shiny / Glossy ☐ Dull

☐ Molted ☐ Waxy ☐ Discolored ☐ Bubbles

☐ Even color ☐ Fine grain ☐ Coarse ☐ Crumbly ☐ Stratified

2. The Snap – the sound.

Breaks: ☐ Sharply (cracking) ☐ Loudly ☐ Quietly ☐ Softly

3. Aroma – the smell.

☐ Roasted: _____ ☐ Nutty: _____ ☐ Caramel: _____

☐ Dairy: _____ ☐ Vanilla: _____ ☐ Fruity: _____

☐ Vegetal: _____ ☐ Spice: _____ ☐ Floral: _____

4. Texture – Mouthfeel.

Melts: ☐ Quickly ☐ Slowly

Feels: ☐ Smooth ☐ Creamy ☐ Greasy ☐ Slimy

☐ Hard ☐ Waxy ☐ Graining ☐ Gritty ☐ Powdery

Texture: ☐ Cakelike ☐ Fudgy ☐ Gummy ☐ Sticky ☐ Chewy

5. Flavor & Finish

Flavor Intensity: ☐ DOA ☐ Subtle ☐ Bold

Flavor Profile: [Very sweet] 1 2 3 4 5 6 7 8 9 10 [Very bitter]

☐ sweet ☐ sour ☐ bitter ☐ salty ☐ umami/savory

Flavors: _____

_____

Finish: ☐ Fades quickly ☐ Lingers pleasantly ☐ Won't go away

Recommend for: _____

Notes: _____

_____

Eat it again? ☐ Can't pay me to ☐ Maybe ☐ Sure ☐ Yes, please!

Rating: ☆ ☆ ☆ ☆ ☆

Chocolate Savoring Notes

DATE, OCCASION: _____   COMPANION(S): _____

CHOCOLATIER: _____   LOCATION: _____

CHOCOLATE NAME: _____

CACAO ORIGIN: _____   Cacao _____%

TYPE: □ Dark   □ Semi-Sweet   □ Milk   □ White

□ Specialty Flavor: _____

Category: _____ (Bar, truffle, etc.)

Key Ingredients: _____

Allergy status. Contains: □ Gluten / Wheat   □ Milk

□ Soy   □ Eggs

□ Peanuts   □ Tree Nuts

□ Corn   □ Sesame

□ other: _____

Certifications: □ Fair-Trade   □ Rainforest Alliance

□ USDA Organic   □ Non-GMO Project

□ Gluten-Free   □ Kosher

□ Vegan   □ Paleo

Price: _____   Available at: _____

Label / Graphics: _____

_____

1. Appearance

Color: □ Charcoal Brown □ Mocha □ Caramel □ Ivory

Surface: □ Cloudy □ Smooth □ Shiny / Glossy □ Dull

□ Molted □ Waxy □ Discolored □ Bubbles

□ Even color □ Fine grain □ Coarse □ Crumbly □ Stratified

2. The Snap – the sound.

Breaks: □ Sharply (cracking) □ Loudly □ Quietly □ Softly

3. Aroma – the smell.

□ Roasted: _____ □ Nutty: _____ □ Caramel: _____

□ Dairy: _____ □ Vanilla: _____ □ Fruity: _____

□ Vegetal: _____ □ Spice: _____ □ Floral: _____

4. Texture – Mouthfeel.

Melts: □ Quickly □ Slowly

Feels: □ Smooth □ Creamy □ Greasy □ Slimy

□ Hard □ Waxy □ Graining □ Gritty □ Powdery

Texture: □ Cakelike □ Fudgy □ Gummy □ Sticky □ Chewy

5. Flavor & Finish

Flavor Intensity: □ DOA □ Subtle □ Bold

Flavor Profile: [Very sweet] 1   2   3   4   5   6   7   8   9   10 [Very bitter]

□ sweet □ sour □ bitter □ salty □ umami/savory

Flavors: _____

_____

Finish: □ Fades quickly □ Lingers pleasantly □ Won't go away

Recommend for: _____

Notes: _____

_____

Eat it again? □ Can't pay me to □ Maybe □ Sure □ Yes, please!

Rating: ☆ ☆ ☆ ☆ ☆

Chocolate Savoring Notes

DATE, OCCASION: _____ COMPANION(S): _____

CHOCOLATIER: _____ LOCATION: _____

CHOCOLATE NAME: _____

CACAO ORIGIN: _____ Cacao _____%

TYPE: □ Dark   □ Semi-Sweet   □ Milk   □ White

□ Specialty Flavor: _____

Category: _____ (Bar, truffle, etc.)

Key Ingredients: _____

Allergy status. Contains: □ Gluten / Wheat   □ Milk

□ Soy   □ Eggs

□ Peanuts   □ Tree Nuts

□ Corn   □ Sesame

□ other: _____

Certifications: □ Fair-Trade   □Rainforest Alliance

□ USDA Organic   □ Non-GMO Project

□ Gluten-Free   □ Kosher

□ Vegan   □ Paleo

Price: _____   Available at: _____

Label / Graphics: _____

_____

1. Appearance

Color: □ Charcoal Brown □ Mocha □ Caramel □ Ivory

Surface: □ Cloudy □ Smooth □ Shiny / Glossy □ Dull

□ Molted □ Waxy □ Discolored □ Bubbles

□ Even color □ Fine grain □ Coarse □ Crumbly □ Stratified

2. The Snap – the sound.

Breaks: □ Sharply (cracking) □ Loudly □ Quietly □ Softly

3. Aroma – the smell.

□ Roasted: _____ □ Nutty: _____ □ Caramel: _____

□ Dairy: _____ □ Vanilla: _____ □ Fruity: _____

□ Vegetal: _____ □ Spice: _____ □ Floral: _____

4. Texture – Mouthfeel.

Melts: □ Quickly □ Slowly

Feels: □ Smooth □ Creamy □ Greasy □ Slimy

□ Hard □ Waxy □ Graining □ Gritty □ Powdery

Texture: □ Cakelike □ Fudgy □ Gummy □ Sticky □ Chewy

5. Flavor & Finish

Flavor Intensity: □ DOA □ Subtle □ Bold

Flavor Profile: [Very sweet] 1   2   3   4   5   6   7   8   9   10 [Very bitter]

□ sweet □ sour □ bitter □ salty □ umami/savory

Flavors: _____

_____

Finish: □ Fades quickly □ Lingers pleasantly □ Won't go away

Recommend for: _____

Notes: _____

_____

Eat it again? □ Can't pay me to □ Maybe □ Sure □ Yes, please!

Rating: ☆ ☆ ☆ ☆ ☆

Chocolate Savoring Notes

DATE, OCCASION: _____   COMPANION(S): _____

CHOCOLATIER: _____   LOCATION: _____

CHOCOLATE NAME: _____

CACAO ORIGIN: _____   Cacao _____%

TYPE: □ Dark   □ Semi-Sweet   □ Milk   □ White

□ Specialty Flavor: _____

Category: _____ (Bar, truffle, etc.)

Key Ingredients: _____

Allergy status. Contains: □ Gluten / Wheat   □ Milk

□ Soy   □ Eggs

□ Peanuts   □ Tree Nuts

□ Corn   □ Sesame

□ other: _____

Certifications: □ Fair-Trade   □ Rainforest Alliance

□ USDA Organic   □ Non-GMO Project

□ Gluten-Free   □ Kosher

□ Vegan   □ Paleo

Price: _____   Available at: _____

Label / Graphics: _____

_____

1. Appearance

Color: □ Charcoal Brown □ Mocha □ Caramel □ Ivory

Surface: □ Cloudy □ Smooth □ Shiny / Glossy □ Dull

□ Molted □ Waxy □ Discolored □ Bubbles

□ Even color □ Fine grain □ Coarse □ Crumbly □ Stratified

2. The Snap – the sound.

Breaks: □ Sharply (cracking) □ Loudly □ Quietly □ Softly

3. Aroma – the smell.

□ Roasted: _____ □ Nutty: _____ □ Caramel: _____

□ Dairy: _____ □ Vanilla: _____ □ Fruity: _____

□ Vegetal: _____ □ Spice: _____ □ Floral: _____

4. Texture – Mouthfeel.

Melts: □ Quickly □ Slowly

Feels: □ Smooth □ Creamy □ Greasy □ Slimy

□ Hard □ Waxy □ Graining □ Gritty □ Powdery

Texture: □ Cakelike □ Fudgy □ Gummy □ Sticky □ Chewy

5. Flavor & Finish

Flavor Intensity: □ DOA □ Subtle □ Bold

Flavor Profile: [Very sweet] 1   2   3   4   5   6   7   8   9   10 [Very bitter]

□ sweet □ sour □ bitter □ salty □ umami/savory

Flavors: _____

_____

Finish: □ Fades quickly □ Lingers pleasantly □ Won't go away

Recommend for: _____

Notes: _____

_____

Eat it again? □ Can't pay me to □ Maybe □ Sure □ Yes, please!

Rating: ☆ ☆ ☆ ☆ ☆

Chocolate Savoring Notes

DATE, OCCASION: _____   COMPANION(S): _____

CHOCOLATIER: _____   LOCATION: _____

CHOCOLATE NAME: _____

CACAO ORIGIN: _____   Cacao _____%

TYPE: □ Dark   □ Semi-Sweet   □ Milk   □ White

      □ Specialty Flavor: _____

Category: _____ (Bar, truffle, etc.)

Key Ingredients: _____

Allergy status. Contains: □ Gluten / Wheat   □ Milk

                                   □ Soy   □ Eggs

                                   □ Peanuts   □ Tree Nuts

                                   □ Corn   □ Sesame

                                   □ other: _____

Certifications: □ Fair-Trade   □Rainforest Alliance

                                □ USDA Organic   □ Non-GMO Project

                                □ Gluten-Free   □ Kosher

                                □ Vegan   □ Paleo

Price: _____   Available at: _____

Label / Graphics: _____

_____

1. Appearance

Color: ☐ Charcoal Brown   ☐ Mocha   ☐ Caramel   ☐ Ivory

Surface: ☐ Cloudy   ☐ Smooth   ☐ Shiny / Glossy   ☐ Dull

           ☐ Molted   ☐ Waxy   ☐ Discolored   ☐ Bubbles

           ☐ Even color ☐ Fine grain ☐ Coarse   ☐ Crumbly   ☐ Stratified

2. The Snap – the sound.

Breaks: ☐ Sharply (cracking)   ☐ Loudly   ☐ Quietly   ☐ Softly

3. Aroma – the smell.

☐ Roasted: _____   ☐ Nutty: _____   ☐ Caramel: _____

☐ Dairy: _____   ☐ Vanilla: _____   ☐ Fruity: _____

☐ Vegetal: _____   ☐ Spice: _____   ☐ Floral: _____

4. Texture – Mouthfeel.

Melts: ☐ Quickly   ☐ Slowly

Feels: ☐ Smooth   ☐ Creamy   ☐ Greasy   ☐ Slimy

         ☐ Hard   ☐ Waxy   ☐ Graining ☐ Gritty   ☐ Powdery

Texture: ☐ Cakelike   ☐ Fudgy   ☐ Gummy ☐ Sticky   ☐ Chewy

5. Flavor & Finish

Flavor Intensity: ☐ DOA   ☐ Subtle   ☐ Bold

Flavor Profile: [Very sweet] 1   2   3   4   5   6   7   8   9   10 [Very bitter]

                     ☐ sweet   ☐ sour   ☐ bitter   ☐ salty   ☐ umami/savory

Flavors: _____

_____

Finish: ☐ Fades quickly   ☐ Lingers pleasantly   ☐ Won't go away

Recommend for: _____

Notes: _____

_____

Eat it again?   ☐ Can't pay me to   ☐ Maybe   ☐Sure   ☐ Yes, please!

Rating: ☆ ☆ ☆ ☆ ☆

Chocolate Savoring Notes

DATE, OCCASION: _____   COMPANION(S): _____

CHOCOLATIER: _____   LOCATION: _____

CHOCOLATE NAME: _____

CACAO ORIGIN: _____   Cacao _____%

TYPE: □ Dark   □ Semi-Sweet   □ Milk   □ White

□ Specialty Flavor: _____

Category: _____ (Bar, truffle, etc.)

Key Ingredients: _____

Allergy status. Contains: □ Gluten / Wheat   □ Milk

□ Soy   □ Eggs

□ Peanuts   □ Tree Nuts

□ Corn   □ Sesame

□ other: _____

Certifications: □ Fair-Trade   □Rainforest Alliance

□ USDA Organic   □ Non-GMO Project

□ Gluten-Free   □ Kosher

□ Vegan   □ Paleo

Price: _____   Available at: _____

Label / Graphics: _____

_____

1. Appearance

Color: □ Charcoal Brown □ Mocha □ Caramel □ Ivory

Surface: □ Cloudy □ Smooth □ Shiny / Glossy □ Dull

□ Molted □ Waxy □ Discolored □ Bubbles

□ Even color □ Fine grain □ Coarse □ Crumbly □ Stratified

2. The Snap – the sound.

Breaks: □ Sharply (cracking) □ Loudly □ Quietly □ Softly

3. Aroma – the smell.

□ Roasted: _____ □ Nutty: _____ □ Caramel: _____

□ Dairy: _____ □ Vanilla: _____ □ Fruity: _____

□ Vegetal: _____ □ Spice: _____ □ Floral: _____

4. Texture – Mouthfeel.

Melts: □ Quickly □ Slowly

Feels: □ Smooth □ Creamy □ Greasy □ Slimy

□ Hard □ Waxy □ Graining □ Gritty □ Powdery

Texture: □ Cakelike □ Fudgy □ Gummy □ Sticky □ Chewy

5. Flavor & Finish

Flavor Intensity: □ DOA □ Subtle □ Bold

Flavor Profile: [Very sweet] 1   2   3   4   5   6   7   8   9   10 [Very bitter]

□ sweet □ sour □ bitter □ salty □ umami/savory

Flavors: _____

_____

Finish: □ Fades quickly □ Lingers pleasantly □ Won't go away

Recommend for: _____

Notes: _____

_____

Eat it again? □ Can't pay me to □ Maybe □ Sure □ Yes, please!

Rating: ☆ ☆ ☆ ☆ ☆

Chocolate Savoring Notes

DATE, OCCASION: _____   COMPANION(S): _____

CHOCOLATIER: _____   LOCATION: _____

CHOCOLATE NAME: _____

CACAO ORIGIN: _____   Cacao _____%

TYPE: □ Dark   □ Semi-Sweet   □ Milk   □ White

               □ Specialty Flavor: _____

Category: _____ (Bar, truffle, etc.)

Key Ingredients: _____

Allergy status. Contains: □ Gluten / Wheat   □ Milk

                              □ Soy   □ Eggs

                              □ Peanuts   □ Tree Nuts

                              □ Corn   □ Sesame

                              □ other: _____

Certifications: □ Fair-Trade   □Rainforest Alliance

                    □ USDA Organic   □ Non-GMO Project

                    □ Gluten-Free   □ Kosher

                    □ Vegan   □ Paleo

Price: _____   Available at: _____

Label / Graphics: _____

_____

1. Appearance

Color: ☐ Charcoal Brown   ☐ Mocha   ☐ Caramel   ☐ Ivory

Surface: ☐ Cloudy   ☐ Smooth   ☐ Shiny / Glossy   ☐ Dull

☐ Molted   ☐ Waxy   ☐ Discolored   ☐ Bubbles

☐ Even color   ☐ Fine grain   ☐ Coarse   ☐ Crumbly   ☐ Stratified

2. The Snap – the sound.

Breaks: ☐ Sharply (cracking)   ☐ Loudly   ☐ Quietly   ☐ Softly

3. Aroma – the smell.

☐ Roasted: _____   ☐ Nutty: _____   ☐ Caramel: _____

☐ Dairy: _____   ☐ Vanilla: _____   ☐ Fruity: _____

☐ Vegetal: _____   ☐ Spice: _____   ☐ Floral: _____

4. Texture – Mouthfeel.

Melts: ☐ Quickly   ☐ Slowly

Feels: ☐ Smooth   ☐ Creamy   ☐ Greasy   ☐ Slimy

☐ Hard   ☐ Waxy   ☐ Graining ☐ Gritty   ☐ Powdery

Texture: ☐ Cakelike   ☐ Fudgy   ☐ Gummy ☐ Sticky   ☐ Chewy

5. Flavor & Finish

Flavor Intensity: ☐ DOA   ☐ Subtle   ☐ Bold

Flavor Profile: [Very sweet] 1   2   3   4   5   6   7   8   9   10 [Very bitter]

☐ sweet ☐ sour   ☐ bitter ☐ salty   ☐ umami/savory

Flavors: _____

_____

Finish: ☐ Fades quickly   ☐ Lingers pleasantly   ☐ Won't go away

Recommend for: _____

Notes: _____

_____

Eat it again?   ☐ Can't pay me to   ☐ Maybe   ☐Sure   ☐ Yes, please!

Rating: ☆ ☆ ☆ ☆ ☆

Chocolate Savoring Notes

DATE, OCCASION: _____   COMPANION(S): _____

CHOCOLATIER: _____   LOCATION: _____

CHOCOLATE NAME: _____

CACAO ORIGIN: _____   Cacao _____ %

TYPE: □ Dark   □ Semi-Sweet   □ Milk   □ White

□ Specialty Flavor: _____

Category: _____ (Bar, truffle, etc.)

Key Ingredients: _____

Allergy status. Contains: □ Gluten / Wheat   □ Milk

□ Soy   □ Eggs

□ Peanuts   □ Tree Nuts

□ Corn   □ Sesame

□ other: _____

Certifications: □ Fair-Trade   □ Rainforest Alliance

□ USDA Organic   □ Non-GMO Project

□ Gluten-Free   □ Kosher

□ Vegan   □ Paleo

Price: _____   Available at: _____

Label / Graphics: _____

_____

1. Appearance

Color: ☐ Charcoal Brown   ☐ Mocha   ☐ Caramel   ☐ Ivory

Surface: ☐ Cloudy   ☐ Smooth   ☐ Shiny / Glossy   ☐ Dull

         ☐ Molted   ☐ Waxy   ☐ Discolored   ☐ Bubbles

         ☐ Even color   ☐ Fine grain   ☐ Coarse   ☐ Crumbly   ☐ Stratified

2. The Snap – the sound.

Breaks: ☐ Sharply (cracking)   ☐ Loudly   ☐ Quietly   ☐ Softly

3. Aroma – the smell.

☐ Roasted: _____   ☐ Nutty: _____   ☐ Caramel: _____

☐ Dairy: _____   ☐ Vanilla: _____   ☐ Fruity: _____

☐ Vegetal: _____   ☐ Spice: _____   ☐ Floral: _____

4. Texture – Mouthfeel.

Melts: ☐ Quickly   ☐ Slowly

Feels: ☐ Smooth   ☐ Creamy   ☐ Greasy   ☐ Slimy

      ☐ Hard   ☐ Waxy   ☐ Graining ☐ Gritty   ☐ Powdery

Texture: ☐ Cakelike   ☐ Fudgy   ☐ Gummy ☐ Sticky   ☐ Chewy

5. Flavor & Finish

Flavor Intensity: ☐ DOA   ☐ Subtle   ☐ Bold

Flavor Profile: [Very sweet] 1   2   3   4   5   6   7   8   9   10 [Very bitter]

                ☐ sweet   ☐ sour   ☐ bitter   ☐ salty   ☐ umami/savory

Flavors: _____

_____

Finish: ☐ Fades quickly   ☐ Lingers pleasantly   ☐ Won't go away

Recommend for: _____

Notes: _____

_____

Eat it again?   ☐ Can't pay me to   ☐ Maybe   ☐Sure   ☐ Yes, please!

Rating: ☆ ☆ ☆ ☆ ☆

Chocolate Savoring Notes

DATE, OCCASION: _____ COMPANION(S): _____

CHOCOLATIER: _____ LOCATION: _____

CHOCOLATE NAME: _____

CACAO ORIGIN: _____ Cacao _____%

TYPE: □ Dark   □ Semi-Sweet   □ Milk   □ White

             □ Specialty Flavor: _____

Category: _____ (Bar, truffle, etc.)

Key Ingredients: _____

Allergy status. Contains: □ Gluten / Wheat   □ Milk

                                 □ Soy   □ Eggs

                                 □ Peanuts   □ Tree Nuts

                                 □ Corn   □ Sesame

                                 □ other: _____

Certifications: □ Fair-Trade   □Rainforest Alliance

                                 □ USDA Organic   □ Non-GMO Project

                                 □ Gluten-Free   □ Kosher

                                 □ Vegan   □ Paleo

Price: _____   Available at: _____

Label / Graphics: _____

_____

1. Appearance

Color: □ Charcoal Brown   □ Mocha   □ Caramel   □ Ivory

Surface: □ Cloudy   □ Smooth   □ Shiny / Glossy   □ Dull

         □ Molted   □ Waxy   □ Discolored   □ Bubbles

         □ Even color   □ Fine grain   □ Coarse   □ Crumbly   □ Stratified

2. The Snap – the sound.

    Breaks: □ Sharply (cracking)   □ Loudly   □ Quietly   □ Softly

3. Aroma – the smell.

□ Roasted: _____   □ Nutty: _____   □ Caramel: _____

□ Dairy: _____   □ Vanilla: _____   □ Fruity: _____

□ Vegetal: _____   □ Spice: _____   □ Floral: _____

4. Texture – Mouthfeel.

   Melts: □ Quickly   □ Slowly

   Feels: □ Smooth   □ Creamy   □ Greasy   □ Slimy

         □ Hard   □ Waxy   □ Graining □ Gritty   □ Powdery

   Texture: □ Cakelike   □ Fudgy   □ Gummy □ Sticky   □ Chewy

5. Flavor & Finish

Flavor Intensity: □ DOA   □ Subtle   □ Bold

Flavor Profile: [Very sweet] 1   2   3   4   5   6   7   8   9   10 [Very bitter]

                   □ sweet   □ sour   □ bitter   □ salty   □ umami / savory

Flavors: _____

_____

Finish: □ Fades quickly   □ Lingers pleasantly   □ Won't go away

Recommend for: _____

Notes: _____

_____

Eat it again?   □ Can't pay me to   □ Maybe   □Sure   □ Yes, please!

Rating: ☆ ☆ ☆ ☆ ☆

Chocolate Savoring Notes

DATE, OCCASION: _____ COMPANION(S): _____

CHOCOLATIER: _____ LOCATION: _____

CHOCOLATE NAME: _____

CACAO ORIGIN: _____ Cacao _____ %

TYPE: □ Dark □ Semi-Sweet □ Milk □ White

□ Specialty Flavor: _____

Category: _____ (Bar, truffle, etc.)

Key Ingredients: _____

Allergy status. Contains: □ Gluten / Wheat □ Milk

□ Soy □ Eggs

□ Peanuts □ Tree Nuts

□ Corn □ Sesame

□ other: _____

Certifications: □ Fair-Trade □ Rainforest Alliance

□ USDA Organic □ Non-GMO Project

□ Gluten-Free □ Kosher

□ Vegan □ Paleo

Price: _____ Available at: _____

Label / Graphics: _____

_____

1. Appearance

Color: □ Charcoal Brown □ Mocha □ Caramel □ Ivory

Surface: □ Cloudy □ Smooth □ Shiny / Glossy □ Dull

□ Molted □ Waxy □ Discolored □ Bubbles

□ Even color □ Fine grain □ Coarse □ Crumbly □ Stratified

2. The Snap – the sound.

Breaks: □ Sharply (cracking) □ Loudly □ Quietly □ Softly

3. Aroma – the smell.

□ Roasted: _____ □ Nutty: _____ □ Caramel: _____

□ Dairy: _____ □ Vanilla: _____ □ Fruity: _____

□ Vegetal: _____ □ Spice: _____ □ Floral: _____

4. Texture – Mouthfeel.

Melts: □ Quickly □ Slowly

Feels: □ Smooth □ Creamy □ Greasy □ Slimy

□ Hard □ Waxy □ Graining □ Gritty □ Powdery

Texture: □ Cakelike □ Fudgy □ Gummy □ Sticky □ Chewy

5. Flavor & Finish

Flavor Intensity: □ DOA □ Subtle □ Bold

Flavor Profile: [Very sweet] 1 2 3 4 5 6 7 8 9 10 [Very bitter]

□ sweet □ sour □ bitter □ salty □ umami/savory

Flavors: _____

_____

Finish: □ Fades quickly □ Lingers pleasantly □ Won't go away

Recommend for: _____

Notes: _____

_____

Eat it again? □ Can't pay me to □ Maybe □Sure □ Yes, please!

Rating: ☆ ☆ ☆ ☆ ☆

Chocolate Savoring Notes

DATE, OCCASION: _____   COMPANION(S): _____

CHOCOLATIER: _____   LOCATION: _____

CHOCOLATE NAME: _____

CACAO ORIGIN: _____   Cacao _____%

TYPE: □ Dark   □ Semi-Sweet   □ Milk   □ White

          □ Specialty Flavor: _____

Category: _____ (Bar, truffle, etc.)

Key Ingredients: _____

Allergy status. Contains: □ Gluten / Wheat   □ Milk

                              □ Soy   □ Eggs

                              □ Peanuts   □ Tree Nuts

                              □ Corn   □ Sesame

                              □ other: _____

Certifications: □ Fair-Trade   □Rainforest Alliance

                    □ USDA Organic   □ Non-GMO Project

                    □ Gluten-Free   □ Kosher

                    □ Vegan   □ Paleo

Price: _____   Available at: _____

Label / Graphics: _____

_____

1. Appearance

Color: ☐ Charcoal Brown   ☐ Mocha   ☐ Caramel   ☐ Ivory

Surface: ☐ Cloudy   ☐ Smooth   ☐ Shiny / Glossy   ☐ Dull

☐ Molted   ☐ Waxy   ☐ Discolored   ☐ Bubbles

☐ Even color   ☐ Fine grain   ☐ Coarse   ☐ Crumbly   ☐ Stratified

2. The Snap – the sound.

Breaks: ☐ Sharply (cracking)   ☐ Loudly   ☐ Quietly   ☐ Softly

3. Aroma – the smell.

☐ Roasted: _____   ☐ Nutty: _____   ☐ Caramel: _____

☐ Dairy: _____   ☐ Vanilla: _____   ☐ Fruity: _____

☐ Vegetal: _____   ☐ Spice: _____   ☐ Floral: _____

4. Texture – Mouthfeel.

Melts: ☐ Quickly   ☐ Slowly

Feels: ☐ Smooth   ☐ Creamy   ☐ Greasy   ☐ Slimy

☐ Hard   ☐ Waxy   ☐ Graining   ☐ Gritty   ☐ Powdery

Texture: ☐ Cakelike   ☐ Fudgy   ☐ Gummy   ☐ Sticky   ☐ Chewy

5. Flavor & Finish

Flavor Intensity: ☐ DOA   ☐ Subtle   ☐ Bold

Flavor Profile: [Very sweet] 1   2   3   4   5   6   7   8   9   10 [Very bitter]

☐ sweet   ☐ sour   ☐ bitter   ☐ salty   ☐ umami/savory

Flavors: _____

_____

Finish: ☐ Fades quickly   ☐ Lingers pleasantly   ☐ Won't go away

Recommend for: _____

Notes: _____

_____

Eat it again?   ☐ Can't pay me to   ☐ Maybe   ☐Sure   ☐ Yes, please!

Rating: ☆ ☆ ☆ ☆ ☆

Chocolate Savoring Notes

DATE, OCCASION: _____ COMPANION(S):_____

CHOCOLATIER: _____ LOCATION: _____

CHOCOLATE NAME: _____

CACAO ORIGIN: _____ Cacao _____%

TYPE: □ Dark   □ Semi-Sweet   □ Milk   □ White

          □ Specialty Flavor: _____

Category: _____ (Bar, truffle, etc.)

Key Ingredients: _____

Allergy status. Contains: □ Gluten / Wheat   □ Milk

                           □ Soy   □ Eggs

                           □ Peanuts   □ Tree Nuts

                           □ Corn   □ Sesame

                           □ other: _____

Certifications: □ Fair-Trade   □ Rainforest Alliance

                  □ USDA Organic   □ Non-GMO Project

                  □ Gluten-Free   □ Kosher

                  □ Vegan   □ Paleo

Price: _____   Available at: _____

Label / Graphics: _____

_____

1. Appearance

Color: ☐ Charcoal Brown   ☐ Mocha   ☐ Caramel   ☐ Ivory

Surface: ☐ Cloudy   ☐ Smooth   ☐ Shiny / Glossy   ☐ Dull

               ☐ Molted   ☐ Waxy   ☐ Discolored   ☐ Bubbles

               ☐ Even color   ☐ Fine grain   ☐ Coarse   ☐ Crumbly   ☐ Stratified

2. The Snap – the sound.

Breaks: ☐ Sharply (cracking)   ☐ Loudly   ☐ Quietly   ☐ Softly

3. Aroma – the smell.

☐ Roasted: _____   ☐ Nutty: _____   ☐ Caramel: _____

☐ Dairy: _____   ☐ Vanilla: _____   ☐ Fruity: _____

☐ Vegetal: _____   ☐ Spice: _____   ☐ Floral: _____

4. Texture – Mouthfeel.

Melts: ☐ Quickly   ☐ Slowly

Feels: ☐ Smooth   ☐ Creamy   ☐ Greasy   ☐ Slimy

           ☐ Hard   ☐ Waxy   ☐ Graining   ☐ Gritty   ☐ Powdery

Texture: ☐ Cakelike   ☐ Fudgy   ☐ Gummy   ☐ Sticky   ☐ Chewy

5. Flavor & Finish

Flavor Intensity: ☐ DOA   ☐ Subtle   ☐ Bold

Flavor Profile: [Very sweet] 1   2   3   4   5   6   7   8   9   10 [Very bitter]

                       ☐ sweet   ☐ sour   ☐ bitter   ☐ salty   ☐ umami/savory

Flavors: _____

_____

Finish: ☐ Fades quickly   ☐ Lingers pleasantly   ☐ Won't go away

Recommend for: _____

Notes: _____

_____

Eat it again?   ☐ Can't pay me to   ☐ Maybe   ☐Sure   ☐ Yes, please!

Rating: ☆ ☆ ☆ ☆ ☆

Chocolate Savoring Notes

DATE, OCCASION: _____   COMPANION(S): _____

CHOCOLATIER: _____   LOCATION: _____

CHOCOLATE NAME: _____

CACAO ORIGIN: _____   Cacao _____%

TYPE: □ Dark   □ Semi-Sweet   □ Milk   □ White

            □ Specialty Flavor: _____

Category: _____ (Bar, truffle, etc.)

Key Ingredients: _____

Allergy status. Contains: □ Gluten / Wheat   □ Milk

                            □ Soy   □ Eggs

                            □ Peanuts   □ Tree Nuts

                            □ Corn   □ Sesame

                            □ other: _____

Certifications: □ Fair-Trade   □Rainforest Alliance

                    □ USDA Organic   □ Non-GMO Project

                    □ Gluten-Free   □ Kosher

                    □ Vegan   □ Paleo

Price: _____   Available at: _____

Label / Graphics: _____

_____

1. Appearance

Color: ☐ Charcoal Brown   ☐ Mocha   ☐ Caramel   ☐ Ivory

Surface: ☐ Cloudy   ☐ Smooth   ☐ Shiny / Glossy   ☐ Dull

☐ Molted   ☐ Waxy   ☐ Discolored   ☐ Bubbles

☐ Even color   ☐ Fine grain   ☐ Coarse   ☐ Crumbly   ☐ Stratified

2. The Snap – the sound.

Breaks: ☐ Sharply (cracking)   ☐ Loudly   ☐ Quietly   ☐ Softly

3. Aroma – the smell.

☐ Roasted: _____   ☐ Nutty: _____   ☐ Caramel: _____

☐ Dairy: _____   ☐ Vanilla: _____   ☐ Fruity: _____

☐ Vegetal: _____   ☐ Spice: _____   ☐ Floral: _____

4. Texture – Mouthfeel.

Melts: ☐ Quickly   ☐ Slowly

Feels: ☐ Smooth   ☐ Creamy   ☐ Greasy   ☐ Slimy

☐ Hard   ☐ Waxy   ☐ Graining   ☐ Gritty   ☐ Powdery

Texture: ☐ Cakelike   ☐ Fudgy   ☐ Gummy   ☐ Sticky   ☐ Chewy

5. Flavor & Finish

Flavor Intensity: ☐ DOA   ☐ Subtle   ☐ Bold

Flavor Profile: [Very sweet] 1   2   3   4   5   6   7   8   9   10 [Very bitter]

☐ sweet   ☐ sour   ☐ bitter   ☐ salty   ☐ umami/savory

Flavors: _____

_____

Finish: ☐ Fades quickly   ☐ Lingers pleasantly   ☐ Won't go away

Recommend for: _____

Notes: _____

_____

Eat it again?   ☐ Can't pay me to   ☐ Maybe   ☐Sure   ☐ Yes, please!

Rating: ☆ ☆ ☆ ☆ ☆

Chocolate Savoring Notes

DATE, OCCASION: _____   COMPANION(S): _____

CHOCOLATIER: _____   LOCATION: _____

CHOCOLATE NAME: _____

CACAO ORIGIN: _____   Cacao _____%

TYPE: □ Dark   □ Semi-Sweet   □ Milk   □ White

□ Specialty Flavor: _____

Category: _____ (Bar, truffle, etc.)

Key Ingredients: _____

Allergy status. Contains: □ Gluten / Wheat   □ Milk

□ Soy   □ Eggs

□ Peanuts   □ Tree Nuts

□ Corn   □ Sesame

□ other: _____

Certifications: □ Fair-Trade   □ Rainforest Alliance

□ USDA Organic   □ Non-GMO Project

□ Gluten-Free   □ Kosher

□ Vegan   □ Paleo

Price: _____   Available at: _____

Label / Graphics: _____

_____

1. Appearance

Color: ☐ Charcoal Brown ☐ Mocha ☐ Caramel ☐ Ivory

Surface: ☐ Cloudy ☐ Smooth ☐ Shiny / Glossy ☐ Dull

☐ Molted ☐ Waxy ☐ Discolored ☐ Bubbles

☐ Even color ☐ Fine grain ☐ Coarse ☐ Crumbly ☐ Stratified

2. The Snap – the sound.

Breaks: ☐ Sharply (cracking) ☐ Loudly ☐ Quietly ☐ Softly

3. Aroma – the smell.

☐ Roasted: _____ ☐ Nutty: _____ ☐ Caramel: _____

☐ Dairy: _____ ☐ Vanilla: _____ ☐ Fruity: _____

☐ Vegetal: _____ ☐ Spice: _____ ☐ Floral: _____

4. Texture – Mouthfeel.

Melts: ☐ Quickly ☐ Slowly

Feels: ☐ Smooth ☐ Creamy ☐ Greasy ☐ Slimy

☐ Hard ☐ Waxy ☐ Graining ☐ Gritty ☐ Powdery

Texture: ☐ Cakelike ☐ Fudgy ☐ Gummy ☐ Sticky ☐ Chewy

5. Flavor & Finish

Flavor Intensity: ☐ DOA ☐ Subtle ☐ Bold

Flavor Profile: [Very sweet] 1   2   3   4   5   6   7   8   9   10 [Very bitter]

☐ sweet ☐ sour ☐ bitter ☐ salty ☐ umami/savory

Flavors: _____

_____

Finish: ☐ Fades quickly ☐ Lingers pleasantly ☐ Won't go away

Recommend for: _____

Notes: _____

_____

Eat it again? ☐ Can't pay me to ☐ Maybe ☐ Sure ☐ Yes, please!

Rating: ☆ ☆ ☆ ☆ ☆

Chocolate Savoring Notes

DATE, OCCASION: _____   COMPANION(S):_____

CHOCOLATIER: _____   LOCATION: _____

CHOCOLATE NAME: _____

CACAO ORIGIN: _____   Cacao _____%

TYPE: □ Dark   □ Semi-Sweet   □ Milk   □ White

              □ Specialty Flavor: _____

Category: _____ (Bar, truffle, etc.)

Key Ingredients: _____

Allergy status. Contains: □ Gluten / Wheat   □ Milk

                             □ Soy   □ Eggs

                             □ Peanuts   □ Tree Nuts

                             □ Corn   □ Sesame

                             □ other: _____

Certifications: □ Fair-Trade   □Rainforest Alliance

                   □ USDA Organic   □ Non-GMO Project

                   □ Gluten-Free   □ Kosher

                   □ Vegan   □ Paleo

Price: _____   Available at: _____

Label / Graphics: _____

_____

1. Appearance

Color: □ Charcoal Brown □ Mocha □ Caramel □ Ivory

Surface: □ Cloudy □ Smooth □ Shiny / Glossy □ Dull

□ Molted □ Waxy □ Discolored □ Bubbles

□ Even color □ Fine grain □ Coarse □ Crumbly □ Stratified

2. The Snap – the sound.

Breaks: □ Sharply (cracking) □ Loudly □ Quietly □ Softly

3. Aroma – the smell.

□ Roasted: _____   □ Nutty: _____   □ Caramel: _____

□ Dairy: _____   □ Vanilla: _____   □ Fruity: _____

□ Vegetal: _____   □ Spice: _____   □ Floral: _____

4. Texture – Mouthfeel.

Melts: □ Quickly □ Slowly

Feels: □ Smooth □ Creamy □ Greasy □ Slimy

□ Hard □ Waxy □ Graining □ Gritty □ Powdery

Texture: □ Cakelike □ Fudgy □ Gummy □ Sticky □ Chewy

5. Flavor & Finish

Flavor Intensity: □ DOA □ Subtle □ Bold

Flavor Profile: [Very sweet] 1 2 3 4 5 6 7 8 9 10 [Very bitter]

□ sweet □ sour □ bitter □ salty □ umami/savory

Flavors: _____

_____

Finish: □ Fades quickly □ Lingers pleasantly □ Won't go away

Recommend for: _____

Notes: _____

_____

Eat it again? □ Can't pay me to □ Maybe □Sure □ Yes, please!

Rating: ☆ ☆ ☆ ☆ ☆

Chocolate Savoring Notes

DATE, OCCASION: _____ COMPANION(S): _____

CHOCOLATIER: _____ LOCATION: _____

CHOCOLATE NAME: _____

CACAO ORIGIN: _____ Cacao _____%

TYPE: □ Dark   □ Semi-Sweet   □ Milk   □ White

         □ Specialty Flavor: _____

Category: _____ (Bar, truffle, etc.)

Key Ingredients: _____

Allergy status. Contains: □ Gluten / Wheat   □ Milk

                             □ Soy   □ Eggs

                             □ Peanuts   □ Tree Nuts

                             □ Corn   □ Sesame

                             □ other: _____

Certifications: □ Fair-Trade   □ Rainforest Alliance

                   □ USDA Organic   □ Non-GMO Project

                   □ Gluten-Free   □ Kosher

                   □ Vegan   □ Paleo

Price: _____   Available at: _____

Label / Graphics: _____

_____

1. Appearance

Color: ☐ Charcoal Brown   ☐ Mocha   ☐ Caramel   ☐ Ivory

Surface: ☐ Cloudy   ☐ Smooth   ☐ Shiny / Glossy   ☐ Dull

           ☐ Molted   ☐ Waxy   ☐ Discolored   ☐ Bubbles

           ☐ Even color   ☐ Fine grain   ☐ Coarse   ☐ Crumbly   ☐ Stratified

2. The Snap – the sound.

Breaks: ☐ Sharply (cracking)   ☐ Loudly   ☐ Quietly   ☐ Softly

3. Aroma – the smell.

☐ Roasted: _____   ☐ Nutty: _____   ☐ Caramel: _____

☐ Dairy: _____   ☐ Vanilla: _____   ☐ Fruity: _____

☐ Vegetal: _____   ☐ Spice: _____   ☐ Floral: _____

4. Texture – Mouthfeel.

Melts: ☐ Quickly   ☐ Slowly

Feels: ☐ Smooth   ☐ Creamy   ☐ Greasy   ☐ Slimy

           ☐ Hard   ☐ Waxy   ☐ Graining ☐ Gritty   ☐ Powdery

Texture: ☐ Cakelike   ☐ Fudgy   ☐ Gummy ☐ Sticky   ☐ Chewy

5. Flavor & Finish

Flavor Intensity: ☐ DOA   ☐ Subtle   ☐ Bold

Flavor Profile: [Very sweet] 1   2   3   4   5   6   7   8   9   10 [Very bitter]

           ☐ sweet   ☐ sour   ☐ bitter   ☐ salty   ☐ umami/savory

Flavors: _____

_____

Finish: ☐ Fades quickly   ☐ Lingers pleasantly   ☐ Won't go away

Recommend for: _____

Notes: _____

_____

Eat it again?   ☐ Can't pay me to   ☐ Maybe   ☐ Sure   ☐ Yes, please!

Rating: ☆ ☆ ☆ ☆ ☆

Chocolate Savoring Notes

DATE, OCCASION: _____   COMPANION(S): _____

CHOCOLATIER: _____   LOCATION: _____

CHOCOLATE NAME: _____

CACAO ORIGIN: _____   Cacao _____%

TYPE: □ Dark   □ Semi-Sweet   □ Milk   □ White

□ Specialty Flavor: _____

Category: _____ (Bar, truffle, etc.)

Key Ingredients: _____

Allergy status. Contains: □ Gluten / Wheat   □ Milk

□ Soy   □ Eggs

□ Peanuts   □ Tree Nuts

□ Corn   □ Sesame

□ other: _____

Certifications: □ Fair-Trade   □Rainforest Alliance

□ USDA Organic   □ Non-GMO Project

□ Gluten-Free   □ Kosher

□ Vegan   □ Paleo

Price: _____   Available at: _____

Label / Graphics: _____

_____

1. Appearance

Color: ☐ Charcoal Brown   ☐ Mocha   ☐ Caramel   ☐ Ivory

Surface: ☐ Cloudy   ☐ Smooth   ☐ Shiny / Glossy   ☐ Dull

☐ Molted   ☐ Waxy   ☐ Discolored   ☐ Bubbles

☐ Even color   ☐ Fine grain   ☐ Coarse   ☐ Crumbly   ☐ Stratified

2. The Snap – the sound.

Breaks: ☐ Sharply (cracking)   ☐ Loudly   ☐ Quietly   ☐ Softly

3. Aroma – the smell.

☐ Roasted: _____   ☐ Nutty: _____   ☐ Caramel: _____

☐ Dairy: _____   ☐ Vanilla: _____   ☐ Fruity: _____

☐ Vegetal: _____   ☐ Spice: _____   ☐ Floral: _____

4. Texture – Mouthfeel.

Melts: ☐ Quickly   ☐ Slowly

Feels: ☐ Smooth   ☐ Creamy   ☐ Greasy   ☐ Slimy

☐ Hard   ☐ Waxy   ☐ Graining   ☐ Gritty   ☐ Powdery

Texture: ☐ Cakelike   ☐ Fudgy   ☐ Gummy   ☐ Sticky   ☐ Chewy

5. Flavor & Finish

Flavor Intensity: ☐ DOA   ☐ Subtle   ☐ Bold

Flavor Profile: [Very sweet] 1   2   3   4   5   6   7   8   9   10 [Very bitter]

☐ sweet   ☐ sour   ☐ bitter   ☐ salty   ☐ umami/savory

Flavors: _____

_____

Finish: ☐ Fades quickly   ☐ Lingers pleasantly   ☐ Won't go away

Recommend for: _____

Notes: _____

_____

Eat it again?   ☐ Can't pay me to   ☐ Maybe   ☐Sure   ☐ Yes, please!

Rating: ☆ ☆ ☆ ☆ ☆

Chocolate Savoring Notes

DATE, OCCASION: _____   COMPANION(S): _____

CHOCOLATIER: _____   LOCATION: _____

CHOCOLATE NAME: _____

CACAO ORIGIN: _____   Cacao _____%

TYPE: □ Dark   □ Semi-Sweet   □ Milk   □ White

□ Specialty Flavor: _____

Category: _____ (Bar, truffle, etc.)

Key Ingredients: _____

Allergy status. Contains: □ Gluten / Wheat   □ Milk

□ Soy   □ Eggs

□ Peanuts   □ Tree Nuts

□ Corn   □ Sesame

□ other: _____

Certifications: □ Fair-Trade   □ Rainforest Alliance

□ USDA Organic   □ Non-GMO Project

□ Gluten-Free   □ Kosher

□ Vegan   □ Paleo

Price: _____   Available at: _____

Label / Graphics: _____

_____

1. Appearance

Color: □ Charcoal Brown □ Mocha □ Caramel □ Ivory

Surface: □ Cloudy □ Smooth □ Shiny / Glossy □ Dull

□ Molted □ Waxy □ Discolored □ Bubbles

□ Even color □ Fine grain □ Coarse □ Crumbly □ Stratified

2. The Snap – the sound.

Breaks: □ Sharply (cracking) □ Loudly □ Quietly □ Softly

3. Aroma – the smell.

□ Roasted: _____ □ Nutty: _____ □ Caramel: _____

□ Dairy: _____ □ Vanilla: _____ □ Fruity: _____

□ Vegetal: _____ □ Spice: _____ □ Floral: _____

4. Texture – Mouthfeel.

Melts: □ Quickly □ Slowly

Feels: □ Smooth □ Creamy □ Greasy □ Slimy

□ Hard □ Waxy □ Graining □ Gritty □ Powdery

Texture: □ Cakelike □ Fudgy □ Gummy □ Sticky □ Chewy

5. Flavor & Finish

Flavor Intensity: □ DOA □ Subtle □ Bold

Flavor Profile: [Very sweet] 1   2   3   4   5   6   7   8   9   10 [Very bitter]

□ sweet □ sour □ bitter □ salty □ umami/savory

Flavors: _____

_____

Finish: □ Fades quickly □ Lingers pleasantly □ Won't go away

Recommend for: _____

Notes: _____

_____

Eat it again? □ Can't pay me to □ Maybe □ Sure □ Yes, please!

Rating: ☆ ☆ ☆ ☆ ☆

Chocolate Savoring Notes

DATE, OCCASION: _____   COMPANION(S): _____

CHOCOLATIER: _____   LOCATION: _____

CHOCOLATE NAME: _____

CACAO ORIGIN: _____   Cacao _____%

TYPE: □ Dark   □ Semi-Sweet   □ Milk   □ White

□ Specialty Flavor: _____

Category: _____ (Bar, truffle, etc.)

Key Ingredients: _____

Allergy status. Contains: □ Gluten / Wheat   □ Milk

□ Soy   □ Eggs

□ Peanuts   □ Tree Nuts

□ Corn   □ Sesame

□ other: _____

Certifications: □ Fair-Trade   □ Rainforest Alliance

□ USDA Organic   □ Non-GMO Project

□ Gluten-Free   □ Kosher

□ Vegan   □ Paleo

Price: _____   Available at: _____

Label / Graphics: _____

_____

1. Appearance

Color: ☐ Charcoal Brown ☐ Mocha ☐ Caramel ☐ Ivory

Surface: ☐ Cloudy ☐ Smooth ☐ Shiny / Glossy ☐ Dull

☐ Molted ☐ Waxy ☐ Discolored ☐ Bubbles

☐ Even color ☐ Fine grain ☐ Coarse ☐ Crumbly ☐ Stratified

2. The Snap – the sound.

Breaks: ☐ Sharply (cracking) ☐ Loudly ☐ Quietly ☐ Softly

3. Aroma – the smell.

☐ Roasted: _____ ☐ Nutty: _____ ☐ Caramel: _____

☐ Dairy: _____ ☐ Vanilla: _____ ☐ Fruity: _____

☐ Vegetal: _____ ☐ Spice: _____ ☐ Floral: _____

4. Texture – Mouthfeel.

Melts: ☐ Quickly ☐ Slowly

Feels: ☐ Smooth ☐ Creamy ☐ Greasy ☐ Slimy

☐ Hard ☐ Waxy ☐ Graining ☐ Gritty ☐ Powdery

Texture: ☐ Cakelike ☐ Fudgy ☐ Gummy ☐ Sticky ☐ Chewy

5. Flavor & Finish

Flavor Intensity: ☐ DOA ☐ Subtle ☐ Bold

Flavor Profile: [Very sweet] 1 2 3 4 5 6 7 8 9 10 [Very bitter]

☐ sweet ☐ sour ☐ bitter ☐ salty ☐ umami/savory

Flavors: _____

_____

Finish: ☐ Fades quickly ☐ Lingers pleasantly ☐ Won't go away

Recommend for: _____

Notes: _____

_____

Eat it again? ☐ Can't pay me to ☐ Maybe ☐Sure ☐ Yes, please!

Rating: ☆ ☆ ☆ ☆ ☆

Chocolate Savoring Notes

DATE, OCCASION: _____   COMPANION(S): _____

CHOCOLATIER: _____   LOCATION: _____

CHOCOLATE NAME: _____

CACAO ORIGIN: _____   Cacao _____%

TYPE: □ Dark   □ Semi-Sweet   □ Milk   □ White

□ Specialty Flavor: _____

Category: _____ (Bar, truffle, etc.)

Key Ingredients: _____

Allergy status. Contains: □ Gluten / Wheat   □ Milk

□ Soy   □ Eggs

□ Peanuts   □ Tree Nuts

□ Corn   □ Sesame

□ other: _____

Certifications: □ Fair-Trade   □ Rainforest Alliance

□ USDA Organic   □ Non-GMO Project

□ Gluten-Free   □ Kosher

□ Vegan   □ Paleo

Price: _____   Available at: _____

Label / Graphics: _____

_____

1. Appearance

Color: ☐ Charcoal Brown ☐ Mocha ☐ Caramel ☐ Ivory

Surface: ☐ Cloudy ☐ Smooth ☐ Shiny / Glossy ☐ Dull

☐ Molted ☐ Waxy ☐ Discolored ☐ Bubbles

☐ Even color ☐ Fine grain ☐ Coarse ☐ Crumbly ☐ Stratified

2. The Snap – the sound.

Breaks: ☐ Sharply (cracking) ☐ Loudly ☐ Quietly ☐ Softly

3. Aroma – the smell.

☐ Roasted: _____ ☐ Nutty: _____ ☐ Caramel: _____

☐ Dairy: _____ ☐ Vanilla: _____ ☐ Fruity: _____

☐ Vegetal: _____ ☐ Spice: _____ ☐ Floral: _____

4. Texture – Mouthfeel.

Melts: ☐ Quickly ☐ Slowly

Feels: ☐ Smooth ☐ Creamy ☐ Greasy ☐ Slimy

☐ Hard ☐ Waxy ☐ Graining ☐ Gritty ☐ Powdery

Texture: ☐ Cakelike ☐ Fudgy ☐ Gummy ☐ Sticky ☐ Chewy

5. Flavor & Finish

Flavor Intensity: ☐ DOA ☐ Subtle ☐ Bold

Flavor Profile: [Very sweet] 1 2 3 4 5 6 7 8 9 10 [Very bitter]

☐ sweet ☐ sour ☐ bitter ☐ salty ☐ umami/savory

Flavors: _____

_____

Finish: ☐ Fades quickly ☐ Lingers pleasantly ☐ Won't go away

Recommend for: _____

Notes: _____

_____

Eat it again? ☐ Can't pay me to ☐ Maybe ☐ Sure ☐ Yes, please!

Rating: ☆ ☆ ☆ ☆ ☆

Chocolate Savoring Notes

DATE, OCCASION: _____   COMPANION(S):_____

CHOCOLATIER: _____   LOCATION: _____

CHOCOLATE NAME: _____

CACAO ORIGIN: _____   Cacao _____%

TYPE: □ Dark   □ Semi-Sweet   □ Milk   □ White

            □ Specialty Flavor: _____

Category: _____ (Bar, truffle, etc.)

Key Ingredients: _____

Allergy status. Contains: □ Gluten / Wheat   □ Milk

                              □ Soy   □ Eggs

                              □ Peanuts   □ Tree Nuts

                              □ Corn   □ Sesame

                              □ other: _____

Certifications: □ Fair-Trade   □Rainforest Alliance

                         □ USDA Organic   □ Non-GMO Project

                         □ Gluten-Free   □ Kosher

                         □ Vegan   □ Paleo

Price: _____   Available at: _____

Label / Graphics: _____

_____

1. Appearance

Color: □ Charcoal Brown □ Mocha □ Caramel □ Ivory

Surface: □ Cloudy □ Smooth □ Shiny / Glossy □ Dull

□ Molted □ Waxy □ Discolored □ Bubbles

□ Even color □ Fine grain □ Coarse □ Crumbly □ Stratified

2. The Snap – the sound.

Breaks: □ Sharply (cracking) □ Loudly □ Quietly □ Softly

3. Aroma – the smell.

□ Roasted: _____ □ Nutty: _____ □ Caramel: _____

□ Dairy: _____ □ Vanilla: _____ □ Fruity: _____

□ Vegetal: _____ □ Spice: _____ □ Floral: _____

4. Texture – Mouthfeel.

Melts: □ Quickly □ Slowly

Feels: □ Smooth □ Creamy □ Greasy □ Slimy

□ Hard □ Waxy □ Graining □ Gritty □ Powdery

Texture: □ Cakelike □ Fudgy □ Gummy □ Sticky □ Chewy

5. Flavor & Finish

Flavor Intensity: □ DOA □ Subtle □ Bold

Flavor Profile: [Very sweet] 1 2 3 4 5 6 7 8 9 10 [Very bitter]

□ sweet □ sour □ bitter □ salty □ umami / savory

Flavors: _____

_____

Finish: □ Fades quickly □ Lingers pleasantly □ Won't go away

Recommend for: _____

Notes: _____

_____

Eat it again? □ Can't pay me to □ Maybe □ Sure □ Yes, please!

Rating: ☆ ☆ ☆ ☆ ☆

Chocolate Savoring Notes

DATE, OCCASION: _____   COMPANION(S):_____

CHOCOLATIER: _____   LOCATION: _____

CHOCOLATE NAME: _____

CACAO ORIGIN: _____   Cacao _____%

TYPE: □ Dark   □ Semi-Sweet   □ Milk   □ White

□ Specialty Flavor: _____

Category: _____ (Bar, truffle, etc.)

Key Ingredients: _____

Allergy status. Contains: □ Gluten / Wheat   □ Milk

□ Soy   □ Eggs

□ Peanuts   □ Tree Nuts

□ Corn   □ Sesame

□ other: _____

Certifications: □ Fair-Trade   □Rainforest Alliance

□ USDA Organic   □ Non-GMO Project

□ Gluten-Free   □ Kosher

□ Vegan   □ Paleo

Price: _____   Available at: _____

Label / Graphics: _____

_____

1. Appearance

Color: ☐ Charcoal Brown ☐ Mocha ☐ Caramel ☐ Ivory

Surface: ☐ Cloudy ☐ Smooth ☐ Shiny / Glossy ☐ Dull

☐ Molted ☐ Waxy ☐ Discolored ☐ Bubbles

☐ Even color ☐ Fine grain ☐ Coarse ☐ Crumbly ☐ Stratified

2. The Snap – the sound.

Breaks: ☐ Sharply (cracking) ☐ Loudly ☐ Quietly ☐ Softly

3. Aroma – the smell.

☐ Roasted: _____ ☐ Nutty: _____ ☐ Caramel: _____

☐ Dairy: _____ ☐ Vanilla: _____ ☐ Fruity: _____

☐ Vegetal: _____ ☐ Spice: _____ ☐ Floral: _____

4. Texture – Mouthfeel.

Melts: ☐ Quickly ☐ Slowly

Feels: ☐ Smooth ☐ Creamy ☐ Greasy ☐ Slimy

☐ Hard ☐ Waxy ☐ Graining ☐ Gritty ☐ Powdery

Texture: ☐ Cakelike ☐ Fudgy ☐ Gummy ☐ Sticky ☐ Chewy

5. Flavor & Finish

Flavor Intensity: ☐ DOA ☐ Subtle ☐ Bold

Flavor Profile: [Very sweet] 1   2   3   4   5   6   7   8   9   10 [Very bitter]

☐ sweet ☐ sour ☐ bitter ☐ salty ☐ umami/savory

Flavors: _____

_____

Finish: ☐ Fades quickly ☐ Lingers pleasantly ☐ Won't go away

Recommend for: _____

Notes: _____

_____

Eat it again? ☐ Can't pay me to ☐ Maybe ☐ Sure ☐ Yes, please!

Rating: ☆ ☆ ☆ ☆ ☆

Chocolate Savoring Notes

DATE, OCCASION: _____   COMPANION(S):_____

CHOCOLATIER: _____   LOCATION: _____

CHOCOLATE NAME: _____

CACAO ORIGIN: _____   Cacao _____%

TYPE: □ Dark   □ Semi-Sweet   □ Milk   □ White

      □ Specialty Flavor: _____

Category: _____ (Bar, truffle, etc.)

Key Ingredients: _____

Allergy status. Contains: □ Gluten / Wheat   □ Milk

                          □ Soy   □ Eggs

                          □ Peanuts   □ Tree Nuts

                          □ Corn   □ Sesame

                          □ other: _____

Certifications: □ Fair-Trade   □Rainforest Alliance

                     □ USDA Organic   □ Non-GMO Project

                     □ Gluten-Free   □ Kosher

                     □ Vegan   □ Paleo

Price: _____   Available at: _____

Label / Graphics: _____

_____

1. Appearance

Color: □ Charcoal Brown   □ Mocha   □ Caramel   □ Ivory

Surface: □ Cloudy   □ Smooth   □ Shiny / Glossy   □ Dull

□ Molted   □ Waxy   □ Discolored   □ Bubbles

□ Even color □ Fine grain □ Coarse   □ Crumbly   □ Stratified

2. The Snap – the sound.

Breaks: □ Sharply (cracking)   □ Loudly   □ Quietly   □ Softly

3. Aroma – the smell.

□ Roasted: _____   □ Nutty: _____   □ Caramel: _____

□ Dairy: _____   □ Vanilla: _____   □ Fruity: _____

□ Vegetal: _____   □ Spice: _____   □ Floral: _____

4. Texture – Mouthfeel.

Melts: □ Quickly   □ Slowly

Feels: □ Smooth   □ Creamy   □ Greasy   □ Slimy

□ Hard   □ Waxy   □ Graining □ Gritty   □ Powdery

Texture: □ Cakelike   □ Fudgy   □ Gummy □ Sticky   □ Chewy

5. Flavor & Finish

Flavor Intensity: □ DOA   □ Subtle   □ Bold

Flavor Profile: [Very sweet] 1   2   3   4   5   6   7   8   9   10 [Very bitter]

□ sweet □ sour   □ bitter □ salty   □ umami/savory

Flavors: _____

_____

Finish: □ Fades quickly   □ Lingers pleasantly   □ Won't go away

Recommend for: _____

Notes: _____

_____

Eat it again?   □ Can't pay me to   □ Maybe   □ Sure   □ Yes, please!

Rating: ☆ ☆ ☆ ☆ ☆

Chocolate Savoring Notes

Date, Occasion: _____   Companion(s): _____

Chocolatier: _____   Location: _____

Chocolate Name: _____

Cacao Origin: _____   Cacao _____ %

Type: □ Dark   □ Semi-Sweet   □ Milk   □ White

     □ Specialty Flavor: _____

Category: _____ (Bar, truffle, etc.)

Key Ingredients: _____

Allergy status. Contains: □ Gluten / Wheat   □ Milk

         □ Soy   □ Eggs

         □ Peanuts   □ Tree Nuts

         □ Corn   □ Sesame

         □ other: _____

Certifications: □ Fair-Trade   □Rainforest Alliance

         □ USDA Organic   □ Non-GMO Project

         □ Gluten-Free   □ Kosher

         □ Vegan   □ Paleo

Price: _____   Available at: _____

Label / Graphics: _____

_____

1. Appearance

Color: □ Charcoal Brown   □ Mocha   □ Caramel   □ Ivory

Surface: □ Cloudy   □ Smooth   □ Shiny / Glossy   □ Dull

□ Molted   □ Waxy   □ Discolored   □ Bubbles

□ Even color   □ Fine grain   □ Coarse   □ Crumbly   □ Stratified

2. The Snap – the sound.

Breaks: □ Sharply (cracking)   □ Loudly   □ Quietly   □ Softly

3. Aroma – the smell.

□ Roasted: _____   □ Nutty: _____   □ Caramel: _____

□ Dairy: _____   □ Vanilla: _____   □ Fruity: _____

□ Vegetal: _____   □ Spice: _____   □ Floral: _____

4. Texture – Mouthfeel.

Melts: □ Quickly   □ Slowly

Feels: □ Smooth   □ Creamy   □ Greasy   □ Slimy

□ Hard   □ Waxy   □ Graining   □ Gritty   □ Powdery

Texture: □ Cakelike   □ Fudgy   □ Gummy   □ Sticky   □ Chewy

5. Flavor & Finish

Flavor Intensity: □ DOA   □ Subtle   □ Bold

Flavor Profile: [Very sweet] 1   2   3   4   5   6   7   8   9   10 [Very bitter]

□ sweet   □ sour   □ bitter   □ salty   □ umami/savory

Flavors: _____

_____

Finish: □ Fades quickly   □ Lingers pleasantly   □ Won't go away

Recommend for: _____

Notes: _____

_____

Eat it again?   □ Can't pay me to   □ Maybe   □Sure   □ Yes, please!

Rating: ☆ ☆ ☆ ☆ ☆

Chocolate Savoring Notes

DATE, OCCASION: _____ COMPANION(S): _____

CHOCOLATIER: _____ LOCATION: _____

CHOCOLATE NAME: _____

CACAO ORIGIN: _____ Cacao _____%

TYPE: □ Dark   □ Semi-Sweet   □ Milk   □ White

           □ Specialty Flavor: _____

Category: _____ (Bar, truffle, etc.)

Key Ingredients: _____

Allergy status. Contains: □ Gluten / Wheat   □ Milk

                            □ Soy   □ Eggs

                            □ Peanuts   □ Tree Nuts

                            □ Corn   □ Sesame

                            □ other: _____

Certifications: □ Fair-Trade   □ Rainforest Alliance

                     □ USDA Organic   □ Non-GMO Project

                     □ Gluten-Free   □ Kosher

                     □ Vegan   □ Paleo

Price: _____   Available at: _____

Label / Graphics: _____

_____

1. Appearance

Color: □ Charcoal Brown   □ Mocha   □ Caramel   □ Ivory

Surface: □ Cloudy   □ Smooth   □ Shiny / Glossy   □ Dull

       □ Molted   □ Waxy   □ Discolored   □ Bubbles

       □ Even color   □ Fine grain   □ Coarse   □ Crumbly   □ Stratified

2. The Snap – the sound.

Breaks: □ Sharply (cracking)   □ Loudly   □ Quietly   □ Softly

3. Aroma – the smell.

□ Roasted: _____   □ Nutty: _____   □ Caramel: _____

□ Dairy: _____   □ Vanilla: _____   □ Fruity: _____

□ Vegetal: _____   □ Spice: _____   □ Floral: _____

4. Texture – Mouthfeel.

Melts: □ Quickly   □ Slowly

Feels: □ Smooth   □ Creamy   □ Greasy   □ Slimy

       □ Hard   □ Waxy   □ Graining □ Gritty   □ Powdery

Texture: □ Cakelike   □ Fudgy   □ Gummy □ Sticky   □ Chewy

5. Flavor & Finish

Flavor Intensity: □ DOA   □ Subtle   □ Bold

Flavor Profile: [Very sweet] 1   2   3   4   5   6   7   8   9   10 [Very bitter]

       □ sweet   □ sour   □ bitter   □ salty   □ umami/savory

Flavors: _____

_____

Finish: □ Fades quickly   □ Lingers pleasantly   □ Won't go away

Recommend for: _____

Notes: _____

_____

Eat it again?   □ Can't pay me to   □ Maybe   □Sure   □ Yes, please!

Rating: ☆ ☆ ☆ ☆ ☆

Notes:

Notes:

Bibliography

Chocolat. 2000.

Entrepreneur. 8 Oct 2008. (https://www.entrepeneur.com/article/197530 (4 Dec 2019)

Forrest Gump. 1994.

Jefferson, Thomas. Letter to John Adams Nov 27, 1789. http://tjrs.monticello.org/letter/1789 (4 Dec 2019).

Like Water for Chocolate. 1992.

Pollan, Michael. *In Defense of Food: An Eater's Manifesto*. New York: Penguin Press, 2008.

Riordan, Rick. *The Sword of Summer*. Disney Hyperion, 2015.

Rowling, J. K. *Harry Potter and the Prisoner of Azkaban* Seabrook, Jane. *Furry Logic Laugh at Life*. New York: Author A. Levine Books, 1999

Solon, Geraldine. *Chocolicious*. Solstice Publishing, 2011.

Vincent, Rachel. *My Soul to Save*. Harlequin Teen, 2009

Willy Wonka and the Chocolate Factory. 1971 & 2005.

About the Author

Dra. Mena Borges-Gillette is a poet, literary translator and university professor who teaches chocolate history, tasting, and making as well as Laughter Yoga, modern languages and literatures. She is the blogger known as Corn-Free Hippie and creator of LiveFreeAndThrive.space, a website for the Food Allergy and Celiac community offering recipes, reviews and resources.

In her free time, she enjoys spending time with her family, being in nature, experiencing the arts and culinary experimentation and crafting.

Saude, Paz, Amor!

Made in the USA
Monee, IL
05 December 2021

83939349R00104